SHOULD YOU EVER FEEL GUILTY?

by
Frank J. McNulty
and
Edward Wakin

PAULIST PRESS
New York/Ramsey/Toronto

Library of Congress
Catalog Card Number: 78-70627

ISBN: 0-8091-2149-2

Published by Paulist Press
Editorial Office: 1865 Broadway, New York, N.Y. 10023
Business Office: 545 Island Road, Ramsey, N.J. 07446

Printed and bound in the
United States of America

Contents

Introduction

On a sunny September day in Chicago's bustling downtown Loop, a non-descript man stood at a street corner and confronted passersby with a startling accusation. He raised his right arm, and as if standing at the gates of heaven, he pointed straight at oncoming Chicagoans and decreed loudly, "GUILTY!"

The accuser set passersby back on their heels. They looked around confused and confounded, and then couldn't wait to get away from him and his dirty word. At one point, a man exclaimed: "But how did *he* know?"

In recounting that urban judgment day, psychiatrist Karl Menninger raised the questions: Guilty of what? Before whom?[1] Those are the questions, but no snap answers will get rid of the feeling, particularly for those who have breathed in guilt at home, in school, and at church—without thinking twice about it.

For many Catholics, the use and abuse of guilt have given both conscience and Church a bad name. This was made clear one evening after a talk on conscience when a woman stood up and said heatedly: "I am happy to hear this different view of conscience—finally. The only time in all my religious training that I ever heard the word conscience the word *guilty* was in front of it!"

Having moved away from such a very legalistic view of morality, Catholicism is now emphasizing

1

more freedom and more personal responsibility. The accent is being taken off the *don'ts* which surrounded Catholics like barbed wire that would prick them with feelings of guilt. The accent has shifted to a more positive morality.

People are still catching up with the change and no one appears more jolted than middle-aged Catholics. From time to time, angry and bitter, they complain that the way they were taught religion left them laden with unnecessary and excessive burdens of guilt. They blame the Church. On the other hand, they are confounded by the attitudes of teenage sons and daughters who seem to have no sense of guilt. Once again, they blame the Church, this time for not instilling a sense of right and wrong.

With the emergence of the newer moral theology, some Catholics got the impression that guilt was being done away with altogether. They became nervous at the appearance of a younger generation that appears to have no sense of sin, that seems to be doing whatever it pleases without a twinge of guilt. Adults who agonized over missing Mass on Sunday when they were growing up encounter some teenagers who couldn't care less about the obligation. (Even teenagers with strong religious commitments may make a point of purposely missing Mass on Sunday and then attending on Monday.) Complaints about the younger generation are heard repeatedly: "Don't they know what sin is?" "They do whatever they please. Don't they ever feel guilty?" "They don't hesitate to hurt their parents, to hurt each other." "What are they learning in Catholic schools?"

Many Catholics have registered a form of future shock because of the changed approach in dealing with sin. Once, they experienced a Church which laid a great deal of guilt upon them; next they felt that the Church had taken away guilt altogether. For them, it was going from one extreme to another. They jibed at moral theologians, calling a moralist "someone who takes away the sins of the world."

Even a Catholic convert like Marshall McLuhan, who is regarded as a futuristic prophet of the electric age of mass media, takes a very traditional view of what the Catholic Church should be doing. McLuhan feels that the Catholic Church should "shake up our present population," adding: "To do that, you'd have to preach nothing but hellfire. In my lifetime, I have never heard one such sermon from a Catholic pulpit. You know there is one brimstone sermon in Joyce's *A Portrait of the Artist as a Young Man.* A very great one in my judgment."[2]

The celebrated economist E. F. Schumacher, whose reputation spread around the world with his book, *Small Is Beautiful*, has reminded us how sin has become a taboo term. When he inveighed against industrial giantism and wasteful consumption, he reminded us that "man's needs are infinite and infinitude can be achieved only in the spiritual realm, never in the material."[3] Then, Schumacher, who converted to Catholicism at the age of sixty, observed in *A Guide for the Perplexed* published shortly before his death in 1977: "In spite of the modern world's chaos and its suffering, there is hardly a concept more unacceptable to it than the idea of sin. What could be the meaning of sin anyhow? Traditionally, it means 'missing the mark,' as in archery, missing the very purpose of human life on earth, a life that affords unique opportunities for development, a great chance and privilege, as the Buddhists have it, 'hard to obtain.' "[4]

Coming from a different direction, psychiatrist Menninger has weighed in with his concern about *Whatever Became of Sin?* He recalled that when he was a boy "sin was still a serious matter and the word was not a jocular term." Then: "I saw this change: I saw it go. I am afraid I even joined in hailing its going." Menninger argues persuasively for awareness of sin as a source of hope: "If the concept of personal responsibility and answerability for ourselves and for others were to return to common acceptance, hope would return to the world with it."[5]

Poet Archibald MacLeish has gone to the heart of the matter:

Guilt matters. Guilt must always matter.
Unless guilt matters, the whole world is
Meaningless.

Between the extremes of excessive guilt and no guilt, there is a humanly-fulfilling and satisfying view of guilt. There is a sound and sensible place for guilt in the moral life. There is a difference between healthy and unhealthy guilt. There is a role for guilt in the lives of men and women—as servant, but not master. So a middle ground beckons between the complaint that the Catholic Church once made people feel too guilty and the criticism that it now does not make people feel guilty enough. The task—which this book sets for itself—is to put guilt in its place.

1
Guilty or Not

To err is human and to feel guilty is a signal that our consciences are working. But the feeling is not necessarily an accurate sign that we are in the wrong.

We all know what the feeling is like: The gnawing discomfort that we have thought or done something that we shouldn't have. Or the sense that we aren't what we should be. Yet, as theologian Karl Rahner points out, conscience can at times be an uncertain guide. "The conscience," he observes in *Nature and Grace*, "is not automatically infallible; it can easily make mistakes, and it is very difficult to distinguish its voice—the real voice of conscience—from the voice of precipitation, passion, convenience or self-will, or of moral primitiveness."

Because guilt and conscience have run together so easily for many Catholics (though hardly confined to them, as busy psychotherapists can report), anyone who is morally concerned has to examine the sources of guilt. Some people specialize in feeling guilty and also have the knack of spreading discomfort. By contrast, others seem to have a talent for ignoring what is wrong in themselves and in their behavior. Funny thing about guilt: Many times we may be feeling guilty when we shouldn't and not feeling guilty when we should.

Conscience can be a trickster as guilt enters through many different doors, often without our noticing. We can feel guilty for a specific, clear-cut violation of a moral responsibility, or we can have a vague sort of uneasiness that floats freely through an aching psyche. We may be conscious of feeling guilty and know WHY. Or we may feel guilty and not know WHY. We can even be unconscious of our guilt feelings as well as their source, yet reveal the feelings indirectly in the way we seek punishment, have forebodings of disaster, or sabotage ourselves.

Because middle-aged men and women stand between two generations and face responsibilities both for their parents and for their children, they are prime candidates for creeping guilt. They are open to feeling guilty as grown sons and daughters as well as parents. They tend to blame themselves for how their children behave and how their parents feel. No evening with a parish parents' group can pass without a husband or wife getting up and saying, with a choking voice, "I'm a good Catholic and I've lived a good life and I've tried very hard to raise my children as good Catholics. Yet they won't go to Mass anymore."

Often, when you talk to them personally, you find they also feel "guilty" about aging parents, as well. Their parents are getting on in years and are feeling financial pressures. They may be having problems with their health or may be making painful adjustments to the loss of a wife or a husband. Or the parents may just be unhappy—and not above complaining with an undertone of blaming.

This is as appropriate a time as any to insert two reminders about the moral life:

1. My primary responsibility is my own life and

living responsibly toward myself and toward others.

2. I cannot live someone else's life. I cannot make someone else moral nor can I make someone else happy. I can only do the best I can, particularly by the examples of my own life.

This does not take us off the hook. It means that we should be as clear-eyed as possible in looking at our own behavior and that of others and that we should learn just when to take responsibility and when not to. For guilt can become a habit without being much of a sign about the morality of our lives. Guilt can become a self-indulgent activity and it can be felt with more than a little assistance from family and friends. For instance: Parent to grown son or daughter: "You didn't even remember to . . ." Grown son or daughter to parent: "If only you had . . ." Or memories of past experiences and actions in family, church, and school can trigger guilt feelings—remembering the time that we . . . The tense can be past, present, or even future.

Guilt can be cruel and unnecessary personal punishment or it can be an appropriate reaction that keeps our moral sensitivities alive and well. Where appropriate, guilt is a legitimate and intrinsic part of living a moral life. It reminds us of our responsibilities. If we act irresponsibly, guilt results. We identify the wrong. We feel guilt as moral feedback. We name it and own it and we can establish the basis for self-correction and for moral development.

Guilt can also be inappropriate and illegitimate. So much of growing up involves an escape from misguided warnings, half-truths, and high-handed admonitions that can come from home, neighborhood, friends, and the media. From warnings about disappointing God and going to hell to fear of making someone sick by misbehaving, the child and the grown adult contend with guilt-laden influences. What is not fully provided from the outside, childhood imagination adds.

In the past—much less so nowadays—Confession could become a triggering device for reviving guilt feelings about things that should have been dead and buried. This was stimulated by what is now an outmoded pastoral practice of encouraging Catholics to present "matter" in the confessional so there would be something to forgive. If penitents had no serious sins in the present, a confessor would ask them about sins of their past life. This led some Catholics to take the very legalistic view of the confessional as the place where you went to have everything washed away. They would include sins of the past and goad themselves into feeling guilty once again, instead of enjoying the merciful love of God. Instead of a place to be healed, for some the confessional became a place to open old wounds.

For those with a distorted view of the Sacrament of Reconciliation, the confessional also became a place where they could avoid making moral decisions. Unsure of their ability to make moral decisions and unwilling to rely on themselves, they played it very safe. They turned over making even the most obvious decisions to the priest.

In a familiar example, a penitent would say, "Father, I missed Mass because I was sick."

The priest would answer: "You don't have to bother confessing that because missing Mass is only a sin when you do it deliberately."

"Yes, I know," the penitent would reply, "but I feel better when I tell it."

Society plays its part, too, in inducing guilt feelings. Building in punishment is one way of keeping us in line even when no one is watching. Ours has been called a "guilt culture" to distinguish Western societies from the "shame cultures" of the East. Our ethical norms are so internalized that we can't escape them. Court is always in session: Judge and jury work around the clock, even holding sessions while we sleep.

Other societies where the focus is on shame provide a perspective on our use of guilt. Japan is the obvious example. Anthropologist Ruth Benedict, in her classic study of the Japanese, describes their emphasis on saving face. In *The Chrysanthemum and the Sword*, she quotes the Japanese sayings, "One cultivates self-respect because of society"; "If there were no society one would not need to respect oneself." Thus, actions that Westerners expect people to feel guilty about, the Japanese expect them to feel shame. Their concern is about public knowledge of their acts. So confession does little for them: If the action is secret, they don't feel the pressure to confess; if it is public, private confession can't take away public shame. So instead of ceremonies to remove sin, Japanese ceremonies court good luck. "True shame cultures," Benedict points out, "rely on external sanctions for good behavior, not, as true guilt cultures do, on an internalized conviction of sin."[1]

All Americans have felt the influence of Puritanism which built morality on guilt. Coming out of England into New England, the Puritans imposed their view of natural man as entirely vile and corrupt, a plaything of the devil. To them, it was human guilt that kept the devil from having a field day.

Sociologist David Riesman provided an updated label and description of an "inner-directed person" who has a "psychic gyroscope which is set going by his parents and can receive signals later on from other authorities who resemble his parents." The gyroscope pilots such a person through life. "Getting off course, whether in response to inner impulses or to the fluctuating voices of contemporaries, may lead to the feeling of guilt." (By contrast, shame is the psychological punishment for Reisman's tradition-directed person.[2])

The distinctly-Catholic contribution to this guilt-laden influence was Jansenism. Out of France came the heretical view of human nature as radically and intrinsically corrupted by original sin and a religious approach that was harsh and unbending. Its carriers to America were 19th-century Irish clergy who had to attend Jansenistic French seminaries after their own seminaries were closed. When they came to the United States, they brought the Jansenist influence with them, an influence that was still felt to some degree in U.S. seminaries before Vatican II.

Jansenism has been reflected in a view of the Catholic Church which sees it as making laws and building high, barbed-wire fences around its members who would otherwise go astray. The faithful were to be saved from themselves by a stern authoritarian guardian. They could not be left on their own. They could not be trusted to find their own way—a view that is basically against creation and incarnation, against the goodness of human beings. Jansenism was evident in scrupulosity among some pre-Vatican II Catholics. They saw sin where there was no sin, evil where there was no evil. They embraced the letter of the law without regard for its spirit.

In an updated approach toward guilt, two attitudes toward God must be changed and, fortunately, they are changing:

1. *God as Policeman*. This comes out of a very limited awareness of human nature and the dimension of sin. It views humans as errant children who would do all sorts of wrong if it weren't for the cop on the beat. It says that without external forces constantly keeping them in check people would get out of control. It sees human beings as lacking in internal checks and balances, as untrustworthy and irresponsible.

This shortchanges the meaning of grace. Once the Church started to talk of grace as a relationship, we began to emphasize what it means to be loved and warmed by the Trinity. God, our loving Father, is prodigal with his love for us and stands with arms outstretched, always ready for our return. Jesus shares a special life with us and we become his brothers and sisters. The Holy Spirit inspires, guides, directs, and makes us more creative and full of life as we work out our Christian destiny. Thus it is all in the family.

2. *Impossible Ideals*. While every ethical system must include ideals, problems arise when they are unrealistically out of reach. When the path to holiness is not presented with an eye on reality, the average person either writes off the whole thing or picks up guilt when he or she falls short of the "impossible dream." Fortunately, preaching has become more realistic in this regard, but the trend is only recent.

An example of the "impossible dream" was the Holy Family sermon which presented a model of family life completely out of reach and out of touch with reality. The preacher would glowingly describe the life together of Mary, Joseph, and Jesus while out there in the pews parents would squirm and teenagers would smirk. It didn't sound like anything they ever experienced. They thought of arguments over which TV program to watch, how late to stay out, who would borrow the car, the angry exchanges over the bills, the hurt silences, the loud outbursts, the slammed doors. Up there in a remote pulpit, a celibate priest was presenting what sounded to them like impossible ideals. The more conscientious the parents and children, the more likely to feel guilt—unwarranted guilt.

What people in the pew need are reassurances that problems do arise, emotions do flare up, family members do rub each other the wrong way. The important thing about family life is not that it is problem-free and devoid of conflict, but that family love enables the members to make up and start again. Once, to counter family mythmaking, a congregation was told that the priests of the parish were going to name the ideal family. A shiny gold trophy (borrowed from the school's athletic department) was displayed as the award. The congregation was told: "We've gotten together and selected what we priests feel is the ideal family in this parish and we are going to present it to that family." The families who were the most involved in parish life were the most uncomfortable. As they reported later, they said to themselves: "Oh, my God! I hope they don't pick my family." They thought of their ups and downs and of the impossible position they would be in as an ideal family. They were relieved that it was only a pulpit ploy to make this point: Nobody is perfect and yet we tend to preach perfection.

These influences hold back mature, self-directing forms of morality. There has been too much emphasis on laws and not enough attention directed to the values underlying the laws. An obsessive concern with law for its own sake puts the emphasis on looking to the law enforcer, namely the Catholic Church as God's representative.

It would help to recall briefly how this worked in the recent past. The paternalism of the Church was reflected in the way the moral life was broken down into a series of *do's* and *don'ts*. Priests were influenced by the "manual approach" toward right and wrong. As with any manual, those in moral theology were filled with details to cover just about every conceivable situation that would crop up in the confessional. For example, there would be some twenty reasons why a Catholic could be excused from the Sunday Mass obligation. These were meant as working tools for the priest-confessor and right up through the late 1950's just about every priest was trained on these manuals.

What was the spirit of these manuals? It was very negative, casuistic, legalistic. The spirit was bound to infect the pastoral approach of priests and it also filtered down into the catechism teaching of the sisters. So you had Catholics knowing the rules much better than the reasons behind them. Too much letter of the law.

It's too simple to look back with anger or condescension at that approach. Those were different times in a much different world for an American Church living in a narrower, more parochial context. Rather than explain or criticize the past, this brief flashback is designed to indicate the way guilt had a field day. Members of a self-centered Church—feeling beleaguered and being influenced both by Puritanism and Jansenism—worried unremittantly about breaking the rules. From fish on Friday to the boundary lines on sex, the rules were enforced by making people guilt prone.

When the Church began to change some rules, confusion was mixed with guilt. Many who had become comfortable with the manual approach were shocked. They saw their religion being thrown out with Friday abstinence and other well-entrenched rules. Almost in the same words, they asked, "If something could be a mortal sin one week and sinless the next, what rules do we have to obey? Then any rule can be changed and no rules are worth anything. Is anything sacred any more?"

Meanwhile, others were proclaiming the "death of sin" in keeping with the growing permissiveness in modern society. Whereas many in the older generation were feeling "betrayed" by the Church, others in the younger generation were looking elsewhere for their guidelines. They were part of a general shift toward being in step with everyone else in American society, rather than with other Catholics.

The process was aptly labeled as being "other-directed" by Professor Reisman. Americans in general—including Catholics and not just young ones—were shaping their lives according to what others were doing. For them, the important *others* were members of their own group, social class, and community. The cues were coming from outside themselves rather than from the inside.

Looking to the rules was also directed outward, but more than clarity was being sought. The rules were designed to support an internal set of values and principles. Rules were developed to support an internal gyroscope. By contrast, the other-directed process involved a radar screen casting a wide-ranging net to pick up social cues. Instead of an internalized code of inner-directed behavior, the ability to pick up signals was stressed. Alongside controls that came primarily from guilt, abetted by shame, anxiety was added.[3]

As people worry more than in previous generations about being out of step, a new guideline has become pronounced: *Everyone else is doing it.* An immediate, compelling medium enabled everyone to find out quickly what everyone else was doing. Television played informer, adviser, and sermonizer much more effectively than any direct pleas from the pulpit. The audience "saw" for itself from soap opera to network news, from family serials to shoot-em-ups, from documentaries to talk shows—at an average viewing of seven hours per household, per day. It's simplistic to blame it all on television, but it's also disastrous for moral theologians to ignore the "gigantic electronic medicine wagon with a Hollywood cast."

Nor can the sex revolution be overlooked. We can condemn it and denounce the results, but no one can deny its impact. As with every revolution, power shifted, in this case from the ability of organized religion to exercise substantial control over sexual behavior. More and more, the guidelines came from prevailing attitudes and from what everyone else was doing—or seems to be doing.

In this garish picture, norms often come across as garbled, faddish stereotypes, changeable even from one decade to the next. (Even devotees of "open marriage" were switching back to "closed marriage" within one short decade.) Such norms, which are closer to fad than law, shape reactions and inevitably influence behavior.

For the morally and religiously concerned, to outlaw laws is irresponsible. To overdo them is to be morally immature. Laws are guidelines for mature moral behavior and they serve conscience in its concern for morality. Conscience is not meant to serve the law. As the Scriptures counsel us, the Sabbath was made for man, not man for the Sabbath. So with all laws. All are called to say *yes* to God, Christians to stay united to Christ; the purpose of laws in Christianity is to help the faithful maintain that union.

It can't be said too often that law has limitations. It provides directions which call for active participation in how they are applied in specific circumstances. Even as guidelines, laws must be changed, adapted and modified in keeping with the real world. A legal system can in no way adequately express the complex reality of our *yes* to God, which is why there will always be exception to law. At such times, obeying the law can contradict the reason for the law.

This is hardly a new conception of law. As Thomas Aquinas states: "Because the human acts with which law deals are surrounded with particular circumstances which are infinitely variable, it is impossible to establish any law that suffers no exception. Lawmakers observe what generally happens and legislate accordingly. In some instances, to observe the law would violate the equality of justice and hurt the very public welfare which law is meant to serve."[4]

At another point, Aquinas pointed out emphatically that law is not designed to take away freedom. In a commentary on the Scriptural citation—"Where the spirit of the Lord is, there is freedom," Aquinas stated: "A man who acts of his own accord acts freely, but one who is impelled by another is not free. He who avoids evil not because it is evil but because a precept of the

Lord forbids it is not free. On the other hand, he who avoids evil because it is evil is free."

This is what the U.S. bishops meant in their November 1966 pastoral letter when they reminded Catholics that "no one is free to evade his personal responsibility by leaving it entirely to others to make moral judgments." The Church in emphasizing responsibility and freedom is calling Catholics to a mature moral life and to leave behind a juvenile approach toward morality built on laws for their own sake. Prohibitions are only meant to remind us what is wrong; they are *not* wrong because they are prohibited.

When faced with excessive legalism in American Catholicism, some Catholics responded by throwing out the Church with the distorted view of morality. They, in effect, reasoned: This is no way to be a mature Christian. I blame the Catholic Church for this distortion. I will leave this distortion behind by leaving the Church.

It's ironic because they have left a Church that does not exist anymore. It is no longer a Church that says as the authoritarian parent stereotypically says to the recalcitrant child: *Do it because I tell you*. Modern moral theology keeps exploring the reasons behind the law, which sometimes leads into challenging questions about whether the law should exist at all. Moralists are focusing on the reasons behind the laws and on strong values to justify *Thou shalt nots*. Modern moral theologians see themselves less as boundary makers, more as frontier seekers, less as answer givers, more as question askers.

Guilt remains in all this, but it then becomes very serious business. Mature behavior is involved. Laws and institutions are seen in perspective, neither blindly accepted nor blindly rejected. Understanding laws means reaching back into the values behind them and assessing the appropriate role of the religious institution making the laws. This begins the process of putting guilt in its appropriate place. It means realizing that to feel guilty is not the same as being guilty. It raises to a profound level the question of guilty or not. It confronts fundamental choice that subverts or exalts each of us in the human condition.

2
Saints, Poets—And Us

In Thornton Wilder's classic portrayal of every-
day American life, *Our Town*, the heroine revisits her
hometown of Grovers Corners and is saddened by
what she finds. The townspeople, especially her family, seem to be living without conviction and loving
without passion. They look to her like walking dead,
unaware of themselves, of others, of the joy of living.
In a poignant moment that brings the play to a dra-
matic standstill, she asks the stage manager whether
people are ever aware of life while they live it, of the
wonder of every single minute. He answers:

"No—saints and poets, maybe—they do some."

That is the call of Christianity: To try a little saint-
hood and poetry in our lives; to be aware of ourselves,
our way of living, and the call of God's love.

When moral theologians talk of *fundamental option*, they are referring to a lifelong commitment that
arises out of a *yes* or *no* in our deepest selves to the call
of God. This becomes our personal *orientation toward
ourselves, toward life, and toward God*. It is a fundamental choice that directs and organizes our entire life.
This is meaningfully done with awareness, by consciously cultivating the saintly and poetic in our own
unique, particular garden. It is not competitive; it is
personal and unique to each of us. To break that fun-

damental relationship is to sin gravely and to invite profound moral guilt.

This provides the context for discussing sin and for guilt resulting from sin. There are other forms of guilt coming from psychological sources and social conditioning, but they are not religious or moral. There are also, as we have discussed, guilt feelings that arise from experiences with the Church. These are distortions arising from misguided legalism. Knowledge of self and of authentic morality, hopefully, can dispel such distortions.

In terms of a *yes* to God, sin becomes a turning away from that commitment. That is the focus rather than the individual acts which obsess the legalistic approach. The shift frees the conscientious person from the entangling burden of splitting hairs, of trying to identify the elusive point at which some moral boundary was or was not breached, of trying to decide how much was too much or when too little was too little. Here, then, is the grave matter of mortal sin: turning away from God. It is breaking the relationship with God. It does not emerge faintly from fine print; it has the force of thunder and lightning.

The living out of our *yes* to God can be illustrated—in a fanciful diagram—by drawing light bulbs all over a blackboard and a single bold line on the bottom. The bulbs represent individual actions, the single line fundamental option. Life's ongoing task is to connect the single actions with the current flowing from the fundamental option so that it illuminates them.

The stream of life is thereby accepted as good and love becomes central—imbedded for the Christian in the central truths of faith. These values shape the

Christian's attitudes and actions so that a Christian is not merely someone obeying rules and regulations. A Christian is acting out commitment to God by responding to the message of Christ.

In no way does emphasis on fundamental option set up a passive situation, with all responsibility shifted into neutral. It would be perverse to say to ourselves: "Well, I have firmed up my fundamental option. I don't have to be concerned about what I do." The opposite is the case. The option is expressed in a continuous process of thought, action, and prayer. It is lifelong.

A Christian does not string together a series of actions that carry labels, such as *loving*, *just*, *helpful*, *self-sacrificing*. This is like drawing up the positive side of a legalistic ledger, with negatives on the opposite itemized as "sins." Christians infuse their lives with their commitment—consciously. They are aware, and they strive for greater awareness.

Morality calls for facing hard questions: Who am I? What are the meaning and consequences of my actions? What am I becoming?

Guilt feelings can act as reminders that we should pay attention to these questions and provide psychological pain if we are ignoring them. But guilt must be evaluated to see whether it is justified in moral terms. However, that is a negative and passive approach, like waiting for a toothache before taking care of our teeth. The Christian is called to be positive and active.

Prayer, in its manifold dimensions, plays a vital role in the process. It unifies our individual acts so that the whole becomes greater than the parts. This is particularly the case in meditation and contemplation which call us back to our true selves so that we stop, look at our lives, and listen to our selves. We reach out for the significance of what we do and how we do it. We take our bearings, we even make resolutions. We strive to avoid what itself can be sinful—unawareness, a refusal to identify and act on our responsibilities to our neighbors and to God.

"Meditation," as St. Francis of Sales pointed out in his 17th-century *Treatise on the Love of God*, "is no other than an attentive thought, voluntarily reiterated and entertained in the mind, to excite the will to holy and salutary affections and resolutions."

In *No Man Is an Island*, Thomas Merton placed this theme in a compelling modern context:

> Every other man is a piece of myself, for I am a part and a member of mankind. Every Christian is part of my own body, because we are members of Christ. What I do is also done for them and with them and by them. What they do is done in me and by me and for me. But each one of us remains responsible for his own share in the life of the whole body. Charity cannot be what it is supposed to be as long as I do not see that my life represents my own allotment in the life of a whole super-natural organism to which I belong. Only when this truth is absolutely central do other doctrines fit into their proper context. Solitude, humility, self-denial, action and contemplation, the sacraments, the monastic life, the family, war and peace—none of these make sense except in relation to the central reality which is God's love living and acting in those whom He has incorporated in His Christ.[1]

This epitomizes the view of guilt based on violating the lifelong *yes* to the call of God rather than on single acts such as missing Sunday Mass. The gravity of grave matter then becomes manifest. The moment of conversion becomes the instant when awareness emerges, when the individual is converted from a habitual pattern that must be changed. Conversion is, then, a turning around, changing direction that was away from God and moving toward God. It is the prodigal son saying that he will return to his father's house. It is the sinner finally hearing the constant and plaintive cry to "come back to me with all your heart."

Usually for the Christian working at his fundamental option, conversion is not, like Saul, being knocked off a horse. It is a continuous process. The call to repent is a call to awareness so that direction can be changed. We are on our way, drift a bit, and need to get back on course, always alert to drifting tendencies. This is what ashes on the forehead say: Repent and believe the Good News. Be aware of your responsibilities. Renew your good resolutions. Deepen your commitment in the way you live your life.

On the deepest level, every human receives God's invitation to act in the fullness of human nature, including those who do not believe in God. It is part of God's universal will to save all humankind by reaching down into what Vatican II called the most secret core and sanctuary — conscience. This was expressed eloquently by Erich Fromm, speaking as an atheist and as a humanist, but nonetheless filled with what is the fundamental question facing each individual: "Is our main effort to worship power, to make money, to have possessions; or is our main effort the perfection of man in the sense of greater love, greater humility, brotherhood, sharing and being alive every moment?" Fromm, who at the age of 77, still was analyzing himself every day and still finding "new things," counseled "an hour every morning in self-analysis and meditation. Coming at the beginning of the day, that already sets the quality of life to some extent."[2]

In terms of the traditional formula for assessing mortal sin, violation of the fundamental option of saying *yes* to God or opting to say *no* to God constitutes grievous matter. While none of us can ever be certain in life that we are fulfilling our commitment to God, our behavior, our dealings with others, and our whole set of values can reassure us (or conversely give us pause). Our daily lives provide answers to the question of whether we are living out our total Christian commitment. Aware, attentive, concerned, we feel an inner sense of confidence. If we depend on others to convince us that we are fulfilling our commitment, we had better take a searching second look at our lives or at our guilt feelings. At such times, prayer that includes meditation and contemplation is strongly prescribed.

While we can never rest on our laurels, we can feel comfortable that we are moving in the right direction, that we are *becoming*. As described elsewhere by one of the co-authors: "You experience peace, though not at all times; you know joy, though not in the measure you would like. Even with an admission that sin and guilt are part of the reality, you have a clear conscience. Your 'Yes' may not always be a loud, clear shout, sometimes it is a faint whisper, and sometimes it gets caught in your throat. But it is 'Yes.' If Jesus asked about your love the way he asked Peter, you could point to your life and say what he did, 'Lord, you know everything; you know I love you' " (Jn. 21:17).[3]

What, then, of sufficient reflection and full consent of the will, are the other two parts of the traditional formula for assessing mortal sin? Here, too, the modern thinking in moral theology takes a middle ground between two extremes that saw too much or too little freedom. Moralists have always made a distinction between the objective action and the subjective responsibility. But in the past, subjective innocence was not admitted as much as it is today.

In a mechanical view of human behavior, wrongdoing operates on a one-to-one basis. The external act is taken as a reliable expression of what is going on inside a person. What you see is regarded as what is. What comes out of a person is viewed as the result of what is inside, so that if an act is wrong, then the person is bad—and guilty. Moral activity operates like. a vending machine: What comes out tells you what is inside.

Moral theologians no longer take a simplistic view of individual acts. Traditionally, the individual was seen as basically free to act in whatever way he or she wanted in all situations. Only certain strong emotions, such as fear and passion, were seen as interfering with the freedom of the act and therefore affecting the individual's responsibility or guilt.

Actually, there are many different levels of consciousness and many different levels of freedom. The subjective element is being appreciated more and more as well as the reality that we do have different degrees of involvement with different actions. Day-in, day-out actions are done habitually, almost without consciousness. They do come from a certain level of freedom, but we do not advert to them as significant moral decisions.

Often, pangs of guilt will arise when individuals

look back over the way they have been behaving
habitually. A husband may suddenly see how he has
been browbeating his wife, a wife how she has been
rejecting her husband, a parent how he or she has been
crushing a child's ego. The feeling of guilt which comes
from such awareness can herald a moment of conversion away from that behavior. When guilt energizes
positive change, it plays a constructive role. It deals
with the present and it is properly dissipated when
change takes place. When guilt is self-indulgent and
hovers in the past, it can distract us from the need to
change in the present. Guilt is also likely to hang on in
such cases.

But we do not act only out of habit. We also confront choices that we view as important and make our
decisions conscious of their significance. We may
agonize over the moral dimensions and weigh the consequences. We consciously take one route or another.
Our eyes are wide open.

Thus, the degree of involvement is crucial—a
realization that will often reduce our sense of guilt or,
sometimes, increase our sense of guilt. But it will be
guilt in perspective and therefore a basis for moral
growth. The Catholic Church has always been clear on
the point. We can commit objectively what is a very
serious moral act, but that does not automatically
make it a serious moral act—subjectively. The degree
of sin or guilt is related to the degree of awareness of
the person.

While this has always been a clear moral doctrine,
there has been a tendency to overemphasize the external act as the barometer of guilt. Now, moral theologians are pointing out that humans are not as free as
once regarded, particularly in a modern world of so

many influences that are both explicit and implicit, overt and subliminal, unconscious and subconscious.

This does not go along with an extreme view that human beings are absolutely determined that actions are controlled by the unconscious. There is a middle ground between the extremes, between innocence on the grounds of no freedom and guilt on the grounds of complete freedom. The individual is not as free as he or she thinks in freer moments nor as conditioned in more restricted moments as some extremists would claim. In such a view, responsibility for a moral act is complex, and sin is not a simplistic one-to-one proposition.

In dealing with guilt, this calls for the care and nourishment of our conscience. To begin, simple realization that much guilt is not morally justified gets people off in the right direction in dealing with guilt. That direction can be psychological rather than moral. Telling people about this often produces a rush of relief. They realize that they are not the doomed sinners of their gloomy imaginations.

The more developed the conscience the greater the ability to see the difference between *feeling* guilty and *being* guilty. This moves us toward greater moral maturity. Jesuit theologian Louis Monden cites the need to make "a clear *distinction* between the *feeling of guilt* and the *awareness of guilt*." He points out that "the blind warning signal of the feeling of guilt" could have been put "completely out of kilter by all kinds of mistakes in our education or traumatic experiences." And he adds, we may feel intense guilt where none is morally warranted and feel no guilt where serious moral faults are involved.[4]

Dealing with the traditional threefold formula of

grievous matter, sufficient reflection and full consent of the will is not an isolated activity. It is not a recurrent episode whenever Confession looms, as was typically the case in the past, but it becomes part of a process—the process of developing a mature conscience in the context of living out the *yes* to God.

3
The Guilt Fallout

In the recent past, these were typical questions being asked by conscientious Catholics:

Is it sinful to perform such duties as mowing the lawn or washing one's automobile on Sunday?

How sinful is it to use the word "damn"?

Since I am responsible for others, please settle this problem. If I arrive late for Mass on a Sunday or holy day, must I attend another Mass, to make up for what I miss?

Is it sinful to disregard traffic laws, lights, etc.?

Upon arrival home, I discovered that a bank teller had given me $10 more than I was entitled to. I was advised to try to return it. Am I bound to under pain of mortal sin?

Is it sinful to invoke the name of God when excited?

According to current regulations, it is no longer required to abstain from water before the reception of Holy Communion. I thought the Church never changed its mind about sin.

May a Catholic over 21 join the 'Y' with a view to gym activities only?

A long time ago, I committed a sin several

times. But only recently did I find out that it is sinful. In the meantime I have been receiving Holy Communion. Must I now confess that sin?

Is it a sin for a parent to permit his son to caddy on Sunday? I think so, but my wife and sons disagree.

Which is the worse sin—birth control or hysterectomy?

These examples, picked randomly from a priest's question-and-answer column for a popular Catholic magazine of the 1950's, illustrate a pre-Vatican II emphasis on hard-and-fast rules. The questions reflect the attempt to present morality in objective terms and the concern about living by the rules. A rule-book morality predominated and its fallout was guilt.

What the Church supplied the faithful wanted. In the name of principles and sound values, the Catholic Church worked hard to provide clearly-defined rules, regulations, and guidelines. This enabled Catholics to know where they stood—without complications. That's what they asked of that priest-columnist and what they asked in the confessional: Give us the answers. Indeed, a remark sometimes heard among the most militant characterized a self-centered, parochial attitude: *THEY (non-Catholics) have all the questions; WE (Catholics) have all the answers*.

In retrospect, the drawbacks of such an attitude are much more apparent than they once were. Moral questions were simplified and sometimes distorted. Individual responsibility for living a moral life played second fiddle to obeying the rules. Moral decisions were put in the hands of an authority—personified by a priest.

Morality was easier to "learn" because it was a matter of remembering the rules, and easier to "teach." Taking over a conscience is not as demanding an effort as educating one and helping it to mature. Instead of making up their own minds, many Catholics found it easier to let someone else do it for them. But "tell-me-what-to-do" morality came at the price of seldom developing a mature conscience—too high a price in the view of contemporary moral theologians.

When Vatican II came along with its growing emphasis on individual responsibility, many Catholics imbued with a rule-oriented approach felt as though they were suddenly pushed into the water and told to swim—without instructions. Sacrosanct rules—that produced instant guilt when violated—were suddenly changed, even abolished. What was once surrendered to those in authority was put in the hands of the individual. The pendulum swung from paternalism to personal responsibility.

In adjusting, Catholics were forced to take a second look at the rules. Adjustment went further. Cultural customs and habits were placed outside the center of Catholicism, so that some people were complaining that it "was hard to tell a 'good Catholic.' " Probably nothing reflected the growing pains as did the end of Friday abstinence—on which so many seemed to feel Judgment Day depended.

Not even official permission could free some Catholics of the guilt fallout from the rules. When Friday abstinence was in effect, one army family confided that it took an entire year before they felt comfortable "biting into a steak" under the dispensation granted them at a military post. Another example of the hold of Friday abstinence was a professional boxer who came to the rectory for permission to eat a steak on the Friday afternoon before a fight at Madison Square Garden. He was a rough-and-tumble slugger who needed that steak both physically and psychologically. Even with the old manual approach toward moral theology, permission to eat the steak was readily given. As he left relieved, this was his response to a friendly remark about going home and enjoying his steak: "Oh, I could never get a steak at home on Friday. My mother would murder me. I have to go to a diner."

So much energy and attention was tied up in obeying the rules that the spirit behind them was often lost. For instance: Lent. The hair-splitting concern over Lenten fast and abstinence—in themselves a marvelous spiritual preparation—preoccupied many Catholics with the *how-to*. Lenten regulations spelled out eating behavior down to the last ounce and to the extra helping of food in the spirit of Weight Watchers rather than of spiritual preparation.

When the bishops changed the entire approach by leaving Lenten practices up to people themselves, the bottom dropped out of Lent for many of them. The bishops urged Catholics to fast and abstain, to seek out charitable activities, to participate in forty days of preparation for the passion, death, and resurrection, but to work out the details for themselves. Today, when asked whether they do more or less during Lent, Catholics often say less. The hope was that Catholics would do more out of a voluntary spirit and with greater understanding. But, realistically, the change over could not be expected to happen overnight.

The long-standing effort to put both right and wrong into rules and regulations conditioned Catholics to look outside themselves for moral cues. They wanted to look up at a "scoreboard" to see whether the official scorekeeper said "hit" or "error." Catholics tended to feel uncomfortable, even guilty, making up their own consciences when changes in their own circumstances or in the rules dictated changes in behavior. They tended to wait for signals from those in authority for reassurance. When this happened, their own consciences were not maturing. And it is the immature conscience that is the playground of inappropriate guilt.

A "tell-me-what-to-do" mentality held back moral development. The individual depended on rules, which if broken would produce uneasiness and guilt. This called for a trip to the confessional where absolution took it all away—until the next time. Because all this could happen outside the individual, it created a tendency to be dependent. Personal responsibility was readily abdicated the way a child waits for a parent to give the go-ahead, to approve or disapprove.

As both moral theologians and psychologists point out, this is not the self-directing conscience at work. It falls far short of the mature Christian who acts freely out of the fullness of faith and commitment—aware, self-directing, responsive to the message of Christ, personally responsible for loving neighbor as self and for loving God.

At Harvard University, psychologist Lawrence Kohlberg has drawn on a formidable body of research to provide a widely-used diagram of moral development and maturity. Moral theologians find his diagram useful in identifying the goal of mature moral development. Three levels of morality are identified: preconventional, conventional, and post-conventional. Each level, in turn, has two stages. Taken together, they help to draw a map of the origins of guilt.

The first level, pre-conventional morality, revolves around good and bad labels and the consequences. At Stage 1, power determines the moral order and fear of punishment keeps the individual in line. Meaning or value is not involved; it is the child obeying because the parent is bigger, stronger, and ready to punish disobedience. At Stage 2, the individual acts to satisfy needs, to act in whatever way gets desired results. Morality has a marketplace rationale: "You scratch my back and I'll scratch yours." A reference to movie characters illustrates the types involved. An example of Stage 1 morality is Dracula's assistant, Renfield, who did whatever his master commanded, whereas Tom Sawyer exemplified Stage 2. His behavior pursued the rewards.

The second level—conventional morality—is based on conformity, on staying in line. Rather than deal primarily with consequences of actions, individuals emphasize their place in family, group, or nation. At Stage 3, within conventional morality, good behavior becomes what pleases others and what wins approval—what is "nice," what the majority approve. At Stage 4, the focus is on law and order. Those in authority command obedience because they are in authority. Laws are not to be judged, but obeyed. The status quo and the social order are maintained for their own sake. They are there and because they are there they call for observance.

Mary Poppins happily danced and sang her way through Stage 3 on the screen, while in *Bridge on the River Kwai* both the Japanese and British colonels were utterly devoted to law and order. In Kohlberg's view of morality in the U.S., most adult Americans, including a majority of college students, are on this level of conventional morality.

The third level—post-conventional morality—looks to values and principles which hold sway apart from the authority of particular groups or persons. The only soldier who refused to obey orders at the My Lai massacre in Vietnam was on this level, according to interviews conducted by Professor Kohlberg. In Stage 5, the right action is defined in terms of general rights and standards which are acceptable to the whole society. General consensus on what is moral plays a major role. Laws are respected and the legal point of view is regarded as the guide, with this difference in Stage 5: Law is not regarded as frozen, but open to change for the benefit of society.

At Stage 6, the highest level, right and wrong are decisions of conscience in keeping with ethical principles developed and held by the individual. The principles are abstract and ethical, embodied in the Golden Rule. They embody universal principles of justice and equality, of human rights, and of respect for the dignity of human beings as individual persons.

Ralph Nader, who has been called a super-citizen, embodies Stage 5 in his commitment to the legal viewpoint and to changing laws for the benefit of society. He embodies Stage 6 in his commitment to justice as a universal principle. In Nader's words: "I think basically what gives me my drive is a very strong sense of what is unjust. The word *justice* occurs again and again. My parents used it a lot—what was just and what was unjust. They oftentimes went back to the Golden Rule and other basic principles of human interaction and relationship."

In literature and movies, *Billy Budd* dramatizes

moral choice where the heart is in conflict with the head. Ship commander Vere is faced with a killing in which the victim personifies malevolence and the killer innocence. Young sailor Budd who exudes goodness strikes his master-at-arms Claggant in outrage at being falsely accused. When Claggart dies, Captain Vere is bound by the mutiny act to hang a seaman who in time of war strikes a superior, much less cause his death. Vere, responding to the standards he must uphold, decides Billy must be punished by hanging. In personifying a moral conscience in Stage 5, Vere "decides to remain unwithdrawn, to accept the responsibility of the human community by accepting the responsibility of command. His decision to maintain order because of man's blindness is his sacrifice of self to the necessities of moral responsibility historically defined" (as one critic notes).

As do saints, Joan of Arc personified the fullness of Stage 6 with her commitment to personal responsibility and accountability, even when those in authority tried to thwart her. Faced with ruthless interrogation at her rigged trial, she delivered her most brilliant answer when asked whether she was in the state of grace. To say no would put her in league with Satan; to say yes would place her at odds with Church teaching that no one can be certain about this all-important question. Her answer has echoed through history: "If I be not in a state of grace, I pray God bring me into it; if I be in a state of grace, I pray God keep me in it."

None of Kohlberg's stages excludes guilt, but its origins are markedly different. An individual who feels guilty after breaking a law out of fear of punishment differs from someone who violates an internalized value. An individual who does the "right" thing because it is expected by others differs from someone who does the "right" thing because he or she expects it of himself or herself. The latter exemplifies autonomy and personal responsibility.

The Gospel makes it clear in which direction Christians should strive in developing their moral selves. Jesus replied to the Pharisee asking which commandment is the greatest: "You shall love the Lord your God with your whole heart, with your whole soul, and with your mind. This is the greatest and first commandment. The second is like it: You shall love your neighbor as yourself. On these two commandments the whole law is based, and the prophets as well." Here is morality at what has just been diagrammed as Stage 6, the level of mature Christianity, the level at which "doing wrong" appropriately leads to feelings of guilt—whether or not a law is broken.

Laws perform various functions, but they are not the final word. The individual conscience is. Laws may be designed to uphold central values, such as the sacredness of life and the commandment to love, and reflect the understanding of values as developed by previous generations. Or law can represent a response to a contemporary situation. Whichever, no law can cover all conceivable cases and no law can be properly viewed in isolation from the real world.

To know the law is not enough. Understanding it makes law meaningful and a servant of the fulfilling moral life. Law and morality are allies, but they are not one and the same. To make them synonymous is to generate the guilt fallout.

4
Choices of a Different Kind

In the play and movie *Equus*, a psychiatrist tried to cure an unstable stable boy who ran amok and blinded six horses. As he treated the disturbed adolescent, the psychiatrist plumbed the many influences on the youth's personality: family, religion, sex taboos, society, social class, laws. He was struck by the fact that certain moments of the youth's infinite number of experiences acquired a magnetic influence. Certain "moments snap together like magnets forging a chain of shackles." Why, he pondered, are certain particular moments magnetized right at the start and not others? Why did these shape the youth and not these others?

The psychiatrist confronted the mystery of each human personality, its uniqueness, and its ineffable individuality. No two humans ever develop the same way—no two classmates, no two members of the same family, no identical twins. Each comes away with different reactions and with different magnetic moments—even from the same experiences. That WHY confounds us as one person's path to innocence is another's to guilt. What we do know is that the sources are psychological, social, and religious and all of us experience them along with the loss of childhood innocence.

On the psychological level, the sources of guilt reach back to our earliest years when we feared disapproval by our parents. In our infantile imaginations, rejection by parents was a fate literally as bad as death. So we all struggled for approval and feared the consequences of failing to achieve it. In one way or another, from early childhood we became involved with reactions to guilt. Sometimes we would accept the guilty feeling and seek punishment, sometimes project the blame onto others, sometimes rationalize our behavior by finding reasons outside ourselves in circumstances and situations or in the behavior of others.

On the sociological level, society stepped immediately into the picture as soon as we left the house, even if it were only as far as the playground. The people, young and old, surrounding us provided plenty of informal schooling in rules; school weighed in with formal lessons. The specter of "being bad" cast its shadow even as we were unclear on what that specifically meant. From earliest childhood, approval seeking went beyond parents to any number of *others*. We pursued acceptance with enthusiasm and we faced rejection with trepidation. As a "Peanuts" cartoon expressed it one day when Charlie Brown hesitated to say hello to a cute little redhead: "It's hard on a face when it gets laughed in."

On the religious level, God entered the picture when we as children encountered the notion of an all-powerful God. Rules and regulations took on a powerful aura and breaking them carried the overtone of trifling with the heavens above—from which thunder and lightning rain down.

From this stream of experiences and influences came moments that "snap together like magnets," the moments that triggered reactions in thought, word, and deed, the moments that played a part in shaping us. In the case of the stable boy in "Equus," the moments in the past came together in a bizarre piece of behavior that a questing psychiatrist struggled to unravel. As with any serious effort to understand another person, the process reflected back on the observer as well. The psychiatrist in this excruciating excursion into the psyche felt his personal pain of living and pondered his own identity. The pain he felt was like a chain in his mouth and he closed the play by uttering his own cry in the wilderness: "I have now in my mouth this sharp chain and it never comes out."

We all must deal with our individual chain of living and choosing. We all must struggle to achieve self-awareness so that we increase our understanding of the "magnetic moments" that helped to shape us. This is an unraveling process in which the moral theologian can act as a guide in identifying the different levels of ethical response. For to live is to be responsible.

As was evident in the diagram of moral development developed by Professor Kohlberg not all responses are the same. For the Christian, Kohlberg's mapping does not go far enough. Beyond the level of instinct and the moral level, there is the Christian-religious level. There, moral choices of a different kind are made. At that level, the moral life becomes a "vocation" rather than an "obligation."

At the level of instinct, laws are outside the person, who is surrounded by taboos. Ethical rules are instinctive and are produced by the surrounding world and its psychological, sociological, and religious pressures. A taboo mentality predominates and is brought about by human contact and society's influences. Its resemblance to animal conduct is evident in the behavior of house pets, who are conditioned by human contact. Anyone who has owned a dog knows the cowering look and body language of Rover after he has chewed up slippers or snatched food from the dining room table. He "feels" guilty.

Pressures from outside the person impose laws and obligations at the instinctual level. The focus is on an act itself that is wrong. Never mind the circumstances, the motive, the purpose, or the freedom of action, *wrong* is *bad*. The penitent who insists on mentioning that he or she missed Mass on Sunday even though there was a valid reason, such as sickness, is giving in to an instinctual reaction. Guilt is triggered by the feeling that something wrong was done, not by the conviction of acting against conscience. Contrition, then, involves an attempt to escape the consequences. "Confession of the fault, expression of a *firm resolve* to stay henceforth within the limits of law, all this belongs to the conjuring rites," Monden observes. "Both are sincerely meant, not however in the sense of a personal decision, but as an instinctive anxiety reflex: 'I'll never dare do such a thing again, too bad I ever ran that risk.' "

On the moral level, self-realization is the main concern. The "right" action aims at fulfillment as human beings and "wrong" means failure to grow. The person says: "I must be faithful to myself and this means living with healthy self-love, loving my neighbor as myself, and coming to terms with the transcendent reality of an all-powerful God." The Golden Rule prevails.

A humanist, when he does not believe in God, resonates to this level of morality. Erich Fromm responds to Thomas Aquinas in the matter of seeing sin not as "disobedience of irrational authority, but the violation of human *well-being.*" Fromm quotes Aquinas: "God can never be insulted by us, except if we act against our own well-being" and goes on to comment: "To appreciate this position, we must consider that, for Thomas, the human good (*bonum humanum*) is determined neither arbitrarily by purely subjective desires, nor by instinctively given desires ('natural,' in the Stoic sense), nor by God's arbitrary will. It is determined by our rational understanding of human nature and of the norms that, based on this nature, are conducive to our optimum growth and well-being."[2]

Rather than punishment from the outside, the guilty deed itself punishes us by diminishing our humanity. Confrontation does not involve an outside force but our own selves, our deepest self-consciousness. No one needs to tell us that we have done wrong. We know it and the awareness is pain and punishment. "The *confession* of one's guilt adds nothing to the value of the inner self-judgment," Monden points out. "It may be one of the many means used for recovery, because it places one's self-condemnation and steady resolve in the concrete framework of one's moral development within a human community."

The ideal level is the Christian religious one which raises human self-realization to a divine intimacy of love. We say *yes* to God the Father through Jesus and go beyond any coercion from outside or inside ourselves. The entire thrust of life on this level comes from love in the fullness of the present moment—with a touch of the poet and the saint. We say *yes* to God in the profoundest meaning of fundamental option.

Here, the Christian says: "It is unthinkable for me

to sin because God loves me so much and I love God in return. When I do sin, I am saying *no* to God. If and when that happens, there is still the opportunity for real contrition and renewal of my dialogue with God."

So for Christians living their lives to the fullest, the important moral decisions involve saying *yes* or *no* to love. Going beyond the rational awareness of what makes us fully human, Christians see themselves in communion with other humans and with God. In this sense, God is love and Christians share in a loving context. To sin is to refuse God's love and to feel guilt is to feel the lonely torment of having rejected love.

"Religious contrition," Monden notes, "is therefore infinitely more than a search for security from the avenging wrath of an offended power, much more, too, than self-condemnation and a will for restoration. It is an appeal to the *mercy* of the beloved, a certitude that love will accept the guilt which we confidently offer and turn it into a new increase of the love relationship. It is our boldness in converting the fault into a trustful offering of love. The answer to this contrition—for on this level of the meeting of persons a response always comes—is *forgiveness*."

Thus in a creative moment the relationship in love is deepened or if need be restored. Rather than a magical rite, the Sacrament of Reconciliation is the sign that the dialogue of love is being renewed in the relationship with God. This is not as abstract as it may appear. While no Christian can be absolutely certain about the fundamental option of saying *yes* to God, we must live with faith in God's love and trust ourselves.

Actually, we are never free of instinct on the emotional level and should not ignore the intellectual level of morality as much as we strive to concentrate on the deeply-personal Christian religious level. We all slip back into feeling uneasy about doing something that we know intellectually is right action or not doing something when we know we don't have to. Yet, there is that lingering feeling . . . I know I was too sick to go to Mass, BUT . . . I know that I didn't have to bring that up in Confession, BUT . . . I know I have to form my own conscience on birth control, BUT . . . I know I can't force my teenager to go to church, BUT . . .

Even the most sophisticated feel such twinges. Dr. Paul Tournier describes the reaction of a doctor who advised a patient to travel by sea rather than by air for medical reasons. Shortly afterward, he heard that her ship was wrecked. "I assure you," the doctor reported, "that I spent some dreadful days until I learned that my patient was among the survivors." Rationally, the doctor knew he actually would only have been "guilty" if he had not given her the best medical advice, which was to travel by sea. Yet, somehow, he felt responsible, however illogical.[3]

While logic will not erase guilt that is felt deeply on the psychological, instinctual level, it helps to identify symptom and source. The priest in the confessional has close contact with the religiously-scrupulous, taboo-bedeviled conscience that clings to guilty feelings. The confessional can only soothe, but not eradicate the condition when it needs treatment. But we all have twinges of instinctual morality and being aware of them helps to put them in their place, particularly when we consciously work toward the Christian religious level of morality.

In major decisions, all three levels usually enter into the process of deciding what is the right thing to do, as, for example, in the case of parents faced with an unwed daughter's pregnancy. Reacting on the instinctual level, parents can focus on a feeling that their daughter has "sinned" and has disgraced them, thereby deserving to be disowned. If the parents are supported by the opinion of friends and family, they can feel vindicated in such an action. It was "the thing to do." On the moral level, the parents would ask themselves: Am I considering the actual needs of my daughter? What are my feelings and responsibilities toward her and toward her baby? Hasn't she already been punished enough? How should I, as a loving parent, act? How do I, as a responsible person, behave in this situation? Here, if the parents decide they must stand by their daughter, outside pressures to condemn her are pushed aside. They are not controlled by social pressures. On the religious level, the parents feel much more than obligation to stand by their daughter. There is, in fact, no choice to consider. They express their authentic love by accepting her—without thereby approving what she did. They respond out of love for her and for the child she will bear. They ignore social embarrassment, they affirm the vocation of loving others as themselves in the context of Christ's message. Their action is indicative of deep love not only for their daughter but for God as well.

Of course, nothing in the moral life operates as simple cause and effect. We pour all our "magnetic moments" into the process along with an ongoing attention to personal moral development. On and on, the process goes. As Thomas Merton wrote in sharing his meditations: "I cannot make good choices unless I develop a mature and prudent conscience that gives me an accurate account of my motives, my intentions, and my moral acts. The word to be stressed here is mature."

Starting with the level of instinct where conscience involves an anxiety reflex and guilt, a blind feeling of having acted wrongly, we all must continuously move upward to the level of self-awareness of ourselves as humans. At that level, our consciences can lead us astray because of false information, but it must be obeyed. Otherwise, guilt brings the realization that we have violated our own growth and development.

Finally, on the Christian religious level, we seek to follow the law of love as a vocation and feel guilty when we say *no* to God who calls us forth with the twofold commandment of love. Then, as Merton reminds fellow Christians, "we account ourselves happy when we know His will and do it, and realize that the greatest unhappiness is to have no sense of His purposes or His designs either for ourselves or for the rest of the world." Conscience then becomes "the light by which we interpret the will of God in our own lives."[4]

5
The Superego/ Conscience Mixup

At times of difficult moral decision, we turn one way, then another. We face in one direction and feel a rush of desire, then a surge of scruples. We look in another direction and consider what makes sense to us and what makes sense to others. We wonder about what we "feel" like doing, want to do, ought to do, have the right to do.

It is an interior moral dance of sense and sensibility. Often, we are not sure to whose tune we are dancing. Is it conscience clearly identifying right and wrong? Or is it fear of authority, the built-in policeman part of us that is called superego? And those twinges of guilt. Where do they come from?

When a moral decision produces conflicting feelings and judgments, the uncertainty can be painful. It can seem as though we are hesitating at the edge of a cliff, about to make a frightening plunge. Yet there really may be no cliff there at all. It all depends. One question that helps to illuminate the process is: "How would you feel if you had to meet God tonight and you were to tell God that you made this decision?"

Time and again, this revealing answer emerges: "Oh, I'd feel fine about God. But I'd be a little nervous about the Church!"

The person is caught between conscience and superego, between the genuine guidance of conscience which says *yes* or *no* and the authority-fearing superego which triggers guilt as a reflex. Confusion about what is meant by conscience and what is meant by superego causes confusion about guilt. It is the runaway superego that produces unhealthy guilt and depicts morality as living a life of *no's*, whereas conscience belongs to a life of *yes's*, with *no's* thrown in when necessary to serve the *yes* to God.

Superego handcuffs us, conscience is the key to responsible freedom. Superego looks to authority, conscience to the value involved. The former is closed, rigid, unthinking, unbending, the latter is open, flexible, aware of circumstances, able to see action in the fullness of a situation.

Conscience is no mysterious force. It is each person's ability to decide right and wrong in the light of all the circumstances and of one's value system. At its deepest level, conscience is a radical call to freedom, summoning us to love ourselves, others, and God. Each of us is called to co-create with God our own future by opening ourselves—to others in the world and to God. Conscience is then a call to grow, not to draw back behind high walls that cut us off from the world. This is heady stuff, for it breathes in freedom and is tied to the joy of living rather than to the gloom of guilt-laden *no's*.

In separating the voices of superego and conscience, modern theologians are dealing with the profound difference between superego guilt and genuine moral guilt. They are definitely not one and the same. Moral guilt involves fundamental option in the deepest sense of turning *toward* or *away* from God. This is not child's play, making incredible the notion that a ten-year-old can commit serious sin. The child is not at that level of moral decision.

What is happening is that theologians and psychologists are examining each other's work on guilt. Theologians are taking into account superego as identified by psychologists and distinguishing it from moral conscience. Psychologists are taking a closer look at the place of conscience, no longer viewing it as much too elusive and belonging entirely to a religious context. This has changed, particularly with the work of Kohlberg and the celebrated Swiss psychologist Jean Piaget. In fact, by 1968 the National Institute of Child Health and Human Development discussed conscience at their annual congress. On their part, theologians have overcome their concern that any psychological explanation would refute the existence of conscience, as if threatening the very notion of genuine moral guilt. The dialogue that is now taking place recognizes the difference between superego and conscience and the presence of guilt in two different realms.

Psychologists provide a useful diagram of the human psyche in terms of id, ego, and superego as worked out in Freud's celebrated formulation:

The id is the reservoir of instinctual drives that are primitive and irrational. Pleasure-seeking and demanding immediate gratification, the id is controlled by the ego and superego.

The ego, in turn, is the organized, largely conscious sub-division of personality. Whereas the pleasure principle dominates the id, the ego operates on the basis of the reality principle. It acts as mediator among the warring forces of the id, the demands of society, and the facts of the physical world.

The superego "stands over" the ego and is the policeman inside the person. It incorporates moral standards which the child experiences in family life, particularly from parents. It internalizes the role of parents as standard-bearers and carries on for them, controlling the passions and drives of the id. Its powerful weapon is guilt, which springs forward automatically.

Freud pointed out that feelings of guilt can be traced to childhood fears of punishment from parents, "more exactly, fear of losing their love." That need for love, for approval and affection, is a primary, all-powerful drive. Loss of love is experienced as a kind of annihilation; it triggers a feeling of panic. For the child, losing love is like losing life itself so he or she absorbs regulations and restrictions as a matter of self-protection. A censor is built in.

But that censor is not concerned with making moral judgments; it is concerned with the passionate pursuit of love and approval from parents and, later, from other authority figures. Its positive side is the desire for love, its negative side is fear of losing love. It produces guilt as an unconscious reflex action.

Not so with moral conscience. It is recognition of the call to love, of the invitation to love God in loving our neighbor. It is a conscious, ongoing process in which we encounter the value and promise of love and the destructive results of rejecting the invitation to love. Peace comes from answering yes to love.

In contrast with superego as primitive conscience, the Christian conscience operates as a creative force. Theologian Gregory Baum has made the point emphatically: "Jesus has come to save men from their superego. God is not punisher; God saves." |

In a penetrating comparison of superego and conscience, Jesuit theologian John W. Glaser has pointed out that "the superego is far more infallible as a tormentor of failure than as a source of effective motivation."[1] Side by side, here are differences between the two:

Superego commands, conscience invites.

Superego seeks approval out of fear that love will be taken away, conscience expresses love seeking to act.

Superego is self-centered; conscience reaches out for a value.

Superego stands still and does not develop; conscience is dynamic, able to deal with new situations.

Superego looks to authority and to the rule; conscience to the value.

Superego focuses on individual "atomized" acts, conscience views individual acts within a larger picture.

Superego is concerned with the past, conscience with the present and future.

Superego seeks punishment in order to clear the record, conscience seeks making up for past misdeeds only as part of living out the value and commitment.

When adults are alerted to the dangers of a runaway superego confounding their moral lives, they respond, almost rejoice. Not that they want "to get away easy" in the way they live, but because they recognize how superego can distort conscientious pursuit of morality. When a moral theologian admits "I have had to work on my own distorted, overgrown superego," Catholics find it easier to deal with their own internal policeman.

Here are some questions that we can ask ourselves in order to become more aware of the part played by the superego in growing up:

Can we remember childhood anxiety feelings before Confession and relief afterward? Where were those feelings coming from?

Did all our teachers like us? Did it matter? In what way did we react to disapproval from teachers?

Who was our favorite teacher? Why?

If we think back to the strictest person we ever met, was that person on second thought really that strict? What were our reactions to signs of strictness?

Did we ever play hooky from school? What feelings did it produce? If we didn't play hooky, what stopped us?

Did we ever steal from a store? Cheat on an exam? Sneak a smoke against the rules? What reactions were set in motion?

When we did something wrong, did we ever feel we were going to get sick as a result?

Thinking over the answers and reactions to those questions takes us back to the buildup of the powerful voice of the superego. It was helping to control us before our mature conscience could take over. But now we must ask whether the superego stood aside as it should have so conscience could take over.

In one of his childhood recollections, humorist Sam Levenson inserts levity into the heavy-handedness of superego in childhood: "According to my Puritan Jewish upbringing, dissipation of earthly goods was decried and decreed as a sin against man and God. I saw, and in fact still see, the luminescent finger of God pointing down at me through a break in the clouds and heard, and still hear, the awful indictment reverberating through the heavens, 'Hey, you. Hey, kid. Hey, Sammy. What's that you're throwing away. Everybody look at him. Wait until I tell your mother. Will you get it from her! Mrs. Levenson.' "

The luminescent finger of God. A familiar image of conscience. When people unfamiliar with new approaches to moral theology are asked to draw a picture of conscience, that's what they come up with time and again: a finger of God. The finger shakes and says no. That's a picture of superego, not conscience. For conscience, why not a luminous lake reflecting the world and the self or a bright sun shining through clouds?

From time to time, interior dialogue helps us to spot the finger-pointing superego at work. Here, for example, is a conversation one of the authors had with himself in trying to decide whether to attend a wake. It came about when he didn't think he could get away in time from a meeting he had to attend. But the meeting broke up early:

"*Good. I will have a chance to attend that wake.*" (Conscience at work, saying, in effect: "Frank, my friend just lost his father. Go to the wake; it will mean something to him.")

"*Wait a minute. I can't go to that wake. I'm not wearing clerical clothes. Priests don't go to wakes dressed like this.*" (Superego warning about making a "bad" appearance, facing disapproval.)

"*Why not? The important thing is consoling the bereaved. It's an act of charity. Look at Jesus and his example in Scripture, at how good he was to Mary and Martha when Lazarus died. Did he worry about what he was wearing?*" (Conscience back again.)

"What will people think? Remember I was taught that a priest should even carry a hat to a wake. I don't have to do that, but at least I have to wear my clericals." (Superego)

"But I gotta go. I have the time. The family would like to see me there. It will mean a lot to them. I'll probably be the only priest there, since they don't know priests in the parish too well. Go to the wake." (Conscience)

"Well, if I go, maybe no one will recognize me. I can sneak in, say a quiet prayer and sneak out, without declaring myself as a priest." (Superego making a concession, but hanging in there.)

As it turned out, the family asked their priest-friend to come forward and lead the mourners in saying the rosary.

In teaching and talking about guilt, people are obviously helped by hearing such examples. They quickly think of examples in their own lives. They are surprised, often relieved, even enlightened about the process that goes on inside themselves when concerned about *right* and *wrong*. They begin to separate superego and conscience—a relief-producing prelude to putting guilt in perspective.

The rules of the Church serve us best when we make that separation. Otherwise, guilt can get out of hand and the guilt that comes from breaking rules can be out of all proportion, even completely unjustified on a moral level. This was dramatized in the past over the adjustment to the end of Friday abstinence or the permission to drink water before receiving Communion. The superego, as usual, was looking at the rules and the rules only. By contrast, the conscience takes into account the rules, but is primarily concerned about the underlying values.

Rule-book Catholicism can be caricatured as putting on the same level a Saturday habit of taking dirty shirts to the laundry and sins to the confessional. An exaggeration, of course, but an important point to emphasize. There was an attitude that we could move between serious sin and repentance about as quickly as we could change a shirt or blouse. Sin, Repent, Sin, Repent, Sin, Repent makes sense in terms of superego guilt, but not in terms of genuine moral guilt which involves the Christian's fundamental option. Theologian Glaser calls the former the "storm and sunshine phenomenon": An individual breaks a commandment and feels overwhelmed by guilt. With confession, the dark clouds of guilt are replaced by sunny skies. This could become a weekly pattern—without reaching the level of a mature moral process.

Whereas a normal, balanced superego functions in everyone, this discussion aims at more than distinguishing between superego and conscience. The overgrown superego needs to be recognized as a source of torment without motivation to change. It can even block direct contact with the underlying values at stake by keeping a spotlight only on individual acts or absorbing our attention with a vague discomfort. Superego's specialty—torment—can actually distract us from moral growth. If we are preoccupied with "erasing" sins and following the rules, we may never pay enough attention to the values behind the rules. We can avoid taking mature responsibility by just leaving it up to authority to tell us right from wrong. This can put us in a cul-de-sac where we are feeling innocent when we should feel guilty and feeling guilty when we should feel innocent.

We have to ask ourselves tough questions:

Are we obsessed with our individual actions—without seeing them in context, without seeing patterns of behavior and attitude, without looking for their meaning in our lives? Are we only concerned with "erasing" sins?

Or are we—in the spirit of a mature conscience—confronting the invitation to love, to the values involved in saying *yes* to God and to the present and future significance of our actions?

This involves the process of identifying superego and conscience in our moral lives and of separating—rather than mixing—the two. For, to put guilt in its place, the superego must be kept in its place.

6
A Place To Reconcile,
A Time To Celebrate

In the darkness of a football coach's screening room, a football star experienced the meaning of forgiveness, a modern parable of reconciliation. Lance Rentzel later turned the experience into a public confession, sharing it with readers of his book, *When All the Laughter Died in Sorrow.*

For Rentzel, shame and disgrace had come in headlines announcing his arrest for exposing himself before small children. He had to be traded to another team, was freed on the charge, and then was arrested again. He described what happened on the day he faced his teammates in the locker room.

At a pre-Sunday strategy session, he "confessed" in front of the entire team: "I guess you've heard a lot of stories about me during these last few days. I wanna tell you that they're all true. And I feel that since you're my teammates and you're wondering how to handle it, I want you to know that it's true. Everyone makes mistakes and I've made some bad ones. I'm in serious trouble. I don't know what's going to happen."

He got that much out and he started to cry. There in the excruciating silence of the locker room, in the inner world of the hulking heroes of professional football, tears streamed down his face. What made him start crying, he recalled, were tears in the eyes of some of his teammates.

He finished his locker room confession: "I hope you want me to stay on the team and that you'll support me and that you'll consider me a friend because that's all I want to be. That's what I want, above all."

Then the coach, to break the heaviness of the scene, started to show films from the team's last game. As Lance sat in the darkened room and the screen flashed images of passes overthrown, tackles missed, and mistakes made, his teammates—one by one— came over and silently touched him on the shoulder, grabbed his hand or patted him on the back. And he knew he was forgiven.

Life is filled with stories that personify reconciliation, profoundly human manifestations of the theology of forgiveness and of the abiding reality that sin and guilt need not be the end of human frailty. In Catholicism, the confessional is a designated place for reconciliation, but it is life itself that best explains the meaning of being reconciled.

For Christians, guilt is never the end of the story. They can fail and sin, yet know they are loved by a personal God who is waiting to forgive and to accept them back.

This is epitomized in the single phrase that the apostle John is supposed to have repeated again and again in his old age: "God is love." Two thousand years later, theologian Karl Barth turned to a simple child's hymn to express the most important truth he had learned as a Christian: "Jesus loves me; this I know, 'cause the Bible tells me so."

The deep-down feeling that we are forgiven, truly

forgiven, is a liberating experience that should free us from guilt. It is reconciliation wedded to conversion and it calls for celebration. It does not occur only in the confessional, for Catholics seek forgiveness in many different ways—in the Penitential Rite of the Mass, in the Eucharist, in prayer. But it is the sacrament of reconciliation that embodies forgiveness. Its liturgy proclaims this good news, the Easter mystery that is brought to each Christian in a personal moment of individual history. The rite of reconciliation is a signal that overflows with reassurance. It is not guilt-obsessed, but by love possessed.

To focus on guilt is to make the confessional a guilt box where absolution deals mainly with the superego instead of the conscience. This is a misuse and downgrading of Confession and has been, for some Catholics, a justification for drifting away from that sacrament. To them, Confession seemed irrelevant, removed from the realities of life, an encounter that seemed to reduce the complexities of morality to the simplicities of a list of individual acts of commission and omission. And worse, made too little of the future and too much of the past.

Catholics have gradually sensed that they were making the same kinds of Confession that they had made at the age of eight or nine—*I did this four times. I did that seven times.* They felt as though they were reduced to looking for the laws and then counting the number of violations per law.

What was happening was the use of a sacrament to absolve superego guilt. Individuals were going to Confession so that religious authority (personified by a priest) would not punish them by withholding approval and acceptance. With Confession, they felt they were winning back approval. In *A Portrait of the Artist as a Young Man*, James Joyce captured the feelings of superego guilt as they relate to Confession when Stephen Dedalus was confronted with his sense of sinning:

> No escape. He had to confess, to speak out in words what he had done and thought, sin after sin. How? How?
> —Father, I . . .
> The thought slid like a cold shining rapier into his tender flesh: confession. But not there in the chapel of the college. He would confess all, every sin of deed and thought, sincerely: but not there among his school companions. Far away from there in some dark place he would murmur out his own shame: and he besought God humbly not to be offended with him if he did not dare to confess in the college chapel: and in utter abjection he craved forgiveness mutely of the boyish hearts about him.

As a kind of magic wand to take away superego guilt, Confession often focused on individual acts and distracted penitents from the need to deal with a way of life, an outlook, and a process. The Sacrament of Reconciliation calls for a broader point of view. It brings peace and hope. It is the next word in an ongoing dialogue with the Lord, a word of sorrow and forgiveness.

Confession should not be used as a cop-out or evasion; it should be the means by which we confront our moral responsibilities. An example would be an area where two individuals might hurt each other, as in the marriage relationship. The confessional is not the only place to seek forgiveness. It is too easy to tell a priest: "I hurt my spouse four times." The spouse already knows it, but nothing is said to him or her. Instead, the offender goes up to the altar and says three Hail Mary's. But this does not confront the ethical task and the particular situation. Let each seek forgiveness from the other in the real world and seek to change in the future.

For reconciliation to have real significance, we must vault over a guilt-laden past into the present and future. We are called to ask ourselves: What are we going to do to change our future? We are summoned to leave guilt behind and to revel in love. If we think mainly in terms of the confessional as the place to have specific acts erased, then we will tend to ignore our overall moral development.

As a place of reconciliation, the confessional signals a renewed dialogue that places the initiative in the person confessing, not in the priest. Rather than tell a penitent what to do, the priest can appropriately say: "Well, we have just brought all this to the scarament and talked it over and it's a serious problem. You're certainly forgiven and we have spoken the good news to each other that we can sin, fail and be forgiven. Certainly, you must have thoughts about the future. What plans have you been making in regard to the situation?" The confessor is doing what he should be doing within the framework of each person's responsibility to lead a moral life. He is asking what he can do to help, *not giving orders as an authority figure*. He is serving the mature moral conscience rather than interfere with its growth.

This reflects the spirit behind the changes in the

Sacrament of Reconciliation. The focus is not on earning forgiveness or winning over God or using a priest's seemingly-magical powers. The changes stress *discovery*. We discover the forgiveness of a loving God who figuratively stands with extended arms waiting for the Prodigal Son to return.

Nor does turning back to God await confession of sins. That conversion takes place beforehand. We have confronted our turning away from God, felt remorse and guilt, decided to convert with confidence in God's love and forgiveness. The sacrament is the signal of what has taken place between the person and a personal God.

To participate fully in the sacrament we should bring our full, authentic selves. The more real both priest and penitent, the better the sacramental encounter and the more real the presence of Jesus. Priest and penitent concelebrate the good news of forgiveness and they can only fully celebrate by being fully themselves—bringing to the event mind and heart. Thoughts, yes, and feelings, too, the visceral as well as the cerebral—the whole person.

So the sacrament becomes not a place to recite a set piece, but to have a conversation of mutual concern. No meaningful conversation can leave out feelings on either side. For the penitent, there are feelings of joy, sadness, misery, hope, doubt, remorse, and guilt (of all kinds). As to our guilt feelings, the confessor can help to identify the types of guilt we are experiencing. He can be a catalyst who will help us see where our guilt is coming from, but he cannot *tell* us. Nor can he *cure* us of neurotic guilt.

Rather than a moral equivalent of paying bills on the first of the month or making up an income tax return, the Sacrament of Reconciliation can be an exhilarating experience. Not always. The sacrament of forgiveness does not require joy to be valid, but at its best it is a peak Christian experience which overcomes guilt.

From twenty-five years of experience with hearing confessions, here is how the clerical co-author of this book would describe the peak moments for the confessor:

"There are times when I am celebrating this sacrament that I literally feel chills up and down my spine because of the beautiful things that happen. Another human being opens up his or her heart to me and says, 'Here's what is happening inside me, the part of me that really matters. I want to share it with you. Help me to discover God's forgiveness.' At such times, I am filled with inspiration and edification. After I celebrate the rite, I always pray better."

In this framework, the Sacrament of Reconciliation is seen—as it should be—as participation in liturgy not confrontation with moral prosecutor. Granted, this changed awareness is not easy, given past conditioning. We are participating with the priest in a celebration, not making a trip to the guillotine. Celebrating, as Joseph Pintauro points out, involves "the need to explain to each other that we are good . . . to explain who we are and to say yea ceremonially. What happens to the man happens to the whole human running race. Always, there remains this need to explain to each other that we are good. We all have a constant need to be reaffirmed."

The sacrament represents a "comeback" on two levels: personal and communal. We not only re-establish dialogue with God, but we are fully reunited to the community of Christians. The new rite signifies and celebrates both levels. Healthy use of the sacrament does not involve superego guilt, but the real thing—guilt that is reality-based and concerns my role in the community.

Thus, guilt is not taken out of context, but put in perspective, as it should be. To be free is to be responsible, to be moral is to be aware. The sacrament increases our *awareness*, stirs up constructive feelings of guilt which can lead to forgiveness, reconciliation, and conversion. Rather than be frozen in the pain of guilt and rendered passive, we are called to be freely responsible and thereby impelled to take action.

The personal aspect has predominated. The sacrament was a private affair, symbolically conducted in semi-darkness and usually clouded in anonymity. The penitent spoke in words of sin and repentance and heard in return words of forgiveness. In spite of the automatic quality that was common, peace and satisfaction did emerge, but it was almost entirely in terms of the individual. The encounter and the outcome were almost totally one-on-one.

The revised rite seeks to keep the personal but also adds the communal. Sin is social in the obvious sense that it violates our relationships with others. It is also social in the less obvious way that the sinner penalizes the community, taking away our greatest gift, our selves. Sin is a withdrawal; we are not functioning up to our full Christian potential. Sins such as social injustice and racism are easily spotted as communal in consequences, but even the most secret of sins has the same result.

We can sin by being irresponsible members of the community, by turning our backs on need, on the moral aspect of public issues. We can sin by consciously approving organized inhumanity. The new rite calls us to confront the reality, as Thomas Merton has reminded us, that "each one of us remains responsible for his own share in the life of the whole body."

Each of us must work out that responsibility in how we live. It is an individual task, but a universal responsibility. Unfortunately, as was pointed out at one synod by Archbishop Gregoire of Montreal, the past emphasis on personal confession helped to blind people to questions about social justice. The communal dimension in the sacrament has been reaffirmed in order to remind us that we *are* our brother's keeper, even when he or she does not live next door.

In this way, the Sacrament of Reconciliation brings us closer to other people as well as to God. For to cut ourselves off from love is to isolate ourselves from fellow humans as well as from God. To be reconciled is to be reconciled in the spirit of the Son of God who gave his life for humanity.

In this context, the Sacrament of Reconciliation is not merely a way to remove guilt. It is a celebration of the discovery of forgiveness. It is not an ending. It is a beginning of a present and future process of living the moral life, of making decisions based on our fundamental commitment to the twofold commandment of love.

7
Writing Our Own Scripts

The classic film director Serge Eisenstein explained the magic of movie-editing by suggesting that we imagine a closeup of a woman's face twisted in terror. Our attention is focused on the look in her eyes, on her heavy breathing, on her contorted features.

The next scene is all-important.

If a roaring lion is leaping toward her, we share her fright.

If it is a mouse, we laugh.

It is what comes next that counts, whether it's a closeup of a man running frantically in the park or a child lying face down on the grass. Is the man being chased by a pursuer with a gun . . . that shoots bullets or water? Is the child going to get up and play or call for help?

The analogy fits the moral life. In the process of making moral decisions, we decide what comes next. We write the script for our own lives at times of conscious, deliberate choice. In the course of growing up and growing old, it adds up to a unique unfolding of a life. An individual life.

At the closeup moments when we become aware of a major decision, we draw on who we are and what we seek to become. We pull ourselves together in order to decide what we ought to do and what we will do. Such times of decision recur in a lifetime. They are climactic times when we identify a significant issue and consciously make a choice.

Major decisions are cumulative. They make a life. They are best seen not only as times when serious sin is avoided, but as opportunities to do significant good. Here is where the growing emphasis on freedom and responsibility is exhilarating for the committed Christian, though it can also be intimidating at times.

There is no question of ordering up the same script for everyone. Each of us is different no matter how much we have in common. The realistic approach does not present easy answers, but describes the process of confronting moral decisions. Because the process brings us in close touch with ourselves and God—as well as the decision—the outcome should be confidence and a feeling of satisfaction.

Five dimensions are involved, all of them intertwined and interacting. The more conscientiously we incorporate them, the sounder the decision. Instead of facing a diffuse guilt afterward, we are investing in conscientious moral searching beforehand. Instead of an inhibiting post-mortem, we seek a freeing experience that enhances our moral development.

1. *Pray.* Turn to the mystery of Jesus present in us. After all, we are trying to figure out what God wants us to do in a particular situation—God, not someone in human authority, not our parents, spouses, friends, or pastor. God is the reference point for moral decisions made by religiously-involved individuals. This is more than a matter of pious thoughts, it is also a matter of being connected with the transcendent reality in the life of a Christian. Thus, the time of moral decision-making is a time of intensified prayer,

of summoning ourselves to our religious commitment. It is not simply praying for help in the decision. It is praying for its own sake, for its enrichment of our moral life. It is keeping the lines open between us and God.

2. *Get into close contact with the teachings of Jesus in Scripture.* We turn to the source of our basic orientation and our moral stance. We look to Scriptures not as a moral theology guidebook, but to nourish our outlook as Christians. By being steeped in Scriptures, we shape our thinking. By attuning ourselves to the Scriptures, we realize that at times we are called to sacrifice and even heroism. From Scripture, we get what theologian Charles Curran calls our "creation, sin, incarnation, redemption, resurrection destiny." It intensifies our awareness of the Christian way of life, it shows us the way to love, to responsibility and freedom, too. But Scriptures are not a set of directions, anymore than a 19th-century travel book can guide our car through Italy. But it can enable us to appreciate the country's way of life and the people. As a guide, we need the current edition of *Michelin*. So with Scripture, which needs to be placed in a modern context in order to be applied.

3. *Get in touch with our personal human dignity.* At times of moral decisions, we need to remember that there is a human nature with a structure and syntax that speaks to good against evil and announces the worth of each human being. This inevitably leads us to ask: Which option is in keeping with human dignity? Which violates human dignity? Which serves and affirms human dignity? While these questions are not answered easily, facing them raises our concern to a level worthy of a serious decision. In doing so, we

invest ourselves and our total personalities in the process of decision-making.

4. *Consider the family of humankind.* Others—of all faiths and no faith—are also engrossed in the human odyssey at this point in history. We must ask: Is this particular decision or action harmful to the common good? We can probe further and ask: Suppose everyone in similar circumstances followed the course of action I select. What would happen? What would be the consequences to society? Would it damage—or benefit—the common good? Personal good cannot be separated from the good of others. There is no *I* without a *Thou* and a *We*. Morality links us to others rather than pulling us apart. It joins rather than separates. It does not write off this world, it places us squarely in it. Free to be responsible. Responsible for that freedom.

5. *Consider the wisdom of the Christian community.* This is Jesus present in the world, in the teachings of Christianity, in the spirit that dwells within. Once again, the news is good, announcing that we are not alone in our strivings. Others are joining us in the effort to decide, to identify what is moral and to share what is learned. The Spirit speaks through all the people of God even though we don't all have the same role in the final formulation of Church teachings. What the Church says about morality comes from collective concern and shared reflections, not from on high, towering, remote, distant. In a Church of collegiality, there is a steady flow of dialogue, of listening, and of discernment. That is the high tide of wisdom.

So we are not alone, not without assistance, guides and guidance in making moral decisions. Having prayed, having gotten close to the teachings of Jesus, having considered human dignity, having weighed the good of humanity and having consulted the Church's teaching, *I* make *my* moral decision. There is collective support, but the decision is individual. Each writes his or her own script. The November 1966 pastoral letter of the U.S. Bishops said it emphatically: "No one is free to evade his personal responsibility by leaving it entirely to others to make moral judgments."

The problem of too-much or too-little guilt is related to two extremes in moral decision-making. One extreme exaggerates the place of authority, the other dismisses it entirely. The first tends to hand over moral decisions to someone else, to externalize them completely, and to place the individual at the mercy of those in authority. And there are enough authority figures ready to provide answers for someone else, often without reasons.

The other extreme isolates moral decisions from all history, teaching, context, and community. Do-your-own-thing becomes the operating principle, ignoring the context in which morally-responsible action takes place. Teaching authority is thereby viewed as synonymous with coercion, an attitude which is spreading. In its extreme form, this amounts to irresponsibility rather than responsibility.

Here is one source of tension in the Catholic Church today. We have a Church that insists on its authority to teach morality—as it always will and should—but we also have a Church that insists on human freedom. Each individual is called upon to follow his or her own conscience. Accommodating the role of a teaching authority and the responsibilities of freedom is never simple and the accommodation is never more real than in the encounter between Church laws and individual conscience.

When laws enter the marketplace of real life with all its complications and variable circumstances, the individual must approach them in terms of the values they uphold, foster, and perpetuate. It is worth repeating, particularly in regard to guilt feelings, that breaking a law in objective terms does not automatically mean that an individual is *guilty*. Nor does obeying a law automatically mean that an individual should feel *free of guilt*. Laws cannot, do not, and should not cover all cases nor command unthinking obedience.

With great clarity Thomas Aquinas shows how hazardous moral decision-making can be, even in regard to natural law. His division of precepts into primary, secondary, and tertiary still helps us to place our decisions in perspective:

PRIMARY—To do good and avoid evil, a precept with which no one argues.

SECONDARY—Basically, the Ten Commandments encompass this level of precepts.

TERTIARY—Norms, rules, and regulations specify what is right and wrong. To take two areas, murder and adultery, tertiary precepts specify when taking of life is murder, when intercourse is adultery. Taking a life in self-defense is different from taking a life for personal gain. Despite agreement that adultery is wrong, differences have existed on what constitutes adultery, depending on the particular culture and historical period. For example, intercourse between a married man and an unmarried woman was not considered fornication in the Jewish tradition. On this level of the tertiary—as St. Thomas points out—moral decisions become increasingly complex and decreasingly obvious and clear. It means getting down to actual cases involving particular people in specific circumstances.

The individual must work through his or her relationship to laws on the tertiary level. This involves attention not only to the law but to the values being promoted by the law. In making moral decisions, *we must attend both to the spirit and to the letter of the law*.

The Catholic Church has always upheld the role of conscience and the right and obligation to follow an informed conscience. For members of that Church, a conscientious moral decision involves attention to its teaching and concern for the purpose of its laws. The next step is to consider whether a particular type of behavior suits or does not suit the purpose of the law. It does not become a matter of deciding whether or not to break a Church law, but of determining whether and how a law applies in a particular situation.

Inappropriate guilt develops when Catholics do not succeed in working out the relationship between laws and values, when they are not fully comfortable with actions taken on behalf of values. They may still carry hangover superego guilt and worry about not following the law out of fear of religious authority. They then would fall into the trap of "serving the law."

After working through this process to make a serious moral decision, a good sign is a feeling of being at peace with oneself. The conscience is untroubled by guilt. At other times, when peace does not come, we must be wary of where twinges of guilt come from. They may not reflect a genuine moral problem so much as social and psychological conditioning. This does not dismiss the real possibility of moral guilt, but such is not likely if we have attended to the five dimensions of moral decision-making and if we have examined Church laws in terms of values. At some point, we must trust ourselves. If we find that we never trust ourselves in our decisions, then it is advisable to look for sources of guilt outside the moral framework.

Just being aware of superego guilt is salutary. When reminded, people become freer to explore the sources of guilt and alert to hangups that bedevil them. Here, mistaken images of God as the cop on the beat can linger on from childhood, combined with past reactions against parental authority. The Church then may be seen as a harsh, strict, disciplinarian acting as the agent of rigid divine authority. Feeling surrounded in this way, an individual can hardly feel free to make a personal decision when faced with the laws of the Church.

Signs of an authority hangup show up in lesser matters such as the routine Church regulation about receiving the Eucharist only once each day. A parishioner will ask, "Father, can I receive a second time today. I received very early this morning, but now that I am together tonight at this community Mass with the retreat team I would like to receive again. We have been working together and I have become very close to them and would like to join as part of the liturgy in receiving the Eucharist. But I always remember being told you shouldn't go to Communion more than once in a day." There should be no conflict here. It is common teaching that there are reasonable exceptions to the rule.

If we find that we feel guilty in making exceptions to routine regulations, then our guilt with more weighty laws may stem from hangups. When feeling guilty in a particular situation, it is useful to recall and examine other occasions of guilt. We can take a cooler look at them than at an immediate pressing situation and more readily recognize hangups.

By trying to develop a clear sense of the influences on our lives from family, society, school, church, and media we can often identify why we feel uneasy. It could involve our discomfort with authority, our uneasiness about not going along with conventional morality, our hesitation to make a personal decision on how laws apply to us.

We should beware of letting guilt induce a kind of paralysis that makes us fearful of acting. This can interfere with our capacity for relating to people and for living a full Christian life. As a prod to moral behavior, guilt can be useful, but as a force that stifles action, guilt is counter-productive. Then it works against Christian involvement with the world and encourages, instead, lack of involvement and withdrawal.

The Christian has no choice but to be involved, to decide and to act. Among the inspiring letters written by the Protestant theologian Dietrich Bonhoeffer while in a Nazi prison is this reminder: "To be a Christian does not mean to be religious in a particular way, to cultivate some particular form of asceticism (as a sinner, a penitent, or a saint), but to be a man. It is not some religious act which makes a Christian what he is, but participation in the suffering of God in the life of the world."

Such participation built on commitment to God and others can be clouded by inappropriate guilt. Knowing what guilt and sin are all about helps to reduce such guilt and to place it in perspective. This understanding does not automatically wipe out inappropriate guilt, but does help to free us from it.

The matter of appropriate guilt remains, as it must, always in the moral life. We can never escape the question, When should we feel guilty? But we can move forward to its positive side: What makes us feel we are seeking innocence? What are our ethical standards? Who are we?

Awareness of sin and feelings of guilt call us to ourselves. Seen as beginnings rather than endings, the awareness and the feelings can put guilt in its place.

8
What Do We Want?

When the apostles Peter and his brother Andrew started following Jesus around, he confronted them with a blunt question that brought them up short: "*What* do you want?"

Jesus had the Talmudic habit of asking questions, of calling for active participation instead of passive acceptance. He could have offered easy answers which would produce acceptance without involvement. That was not the currency in which he dealt. His call was to the total person and his challenge was to seek the Kingdom of God, not merely accept it.

As theologian Avery Dulles has reminded us, "the life of faith consists in constant probing . . . easy answers are not faith, and faith is no answer except to the man who questions deeply." When we question deeply, we live a life that is aware; when we question deeply, we take moral decision-making seriously. In our final chapter, we will spell out the specific signs that a decision-maker should examine. But before reaching that point, information must be collected.

Consider Professor Sam Hill's song in "Music Man" about successful salesmanship: "You Got To Know the Territory." Or the question asked by the perplexed father in the movie, "Lovers and Other Strangers": "What's the story?" That's what we must all find out—"our own story." That's what we must all get to know—our territory. That's where to start in living a moral life—a realistic and conscientious appraisal of the circumstances that count, that are relevant.

Bearing in mind what has already been discussed as a backdrop, it helps to remember that:

Moral decision-making is neither simple nor easy.

Taking your life in your own hands demands more courage than letting another direct it.

Taking over someone else's conscience is much easier than educating one.

Every individual determines the meaning of each action for himself or herself.

Values take precedence over laws.

Laws have exceptions.

Circumstances can mitigate or drastically alter situations.

An action can be objectively sinful, but subjectively sinless.

A responsible moral decision can differ from official Church teaching.

In this context, someone on the outside of an action—whether friend, spouse, parent, or priest—can be helpful, but not decisive in judging its morality. In the spirit of freedom and responsibility, others help in the search for the right questions, but the mature conscience leaves behind old habits of going to someone in authority to make decisions. Others can provide information and example as well as advice. But others should not and cannot make moral decisions for us.

This process of asking questions and attending to the values behind laws has been evident in the matter of birth control. Since the process relates to the entire moral life of the Christian, this could enlighten Catholics about all moral decision-making. In the case of Church teaching on contraception, the value being promoted is responsible use of sexuality on the psychological and biological levels as well as on the level of family life. In facing the question of what the Church is trying to do in its moral teaching on contraception, husbands and wives must focus on their particular marriages and ask specific questions:

What are our relationships and situations?

How many children do we already have?

Are we being called now to bring another into the world?

What is our relationship like at this moment of our committed life together?

What are our obligations to the children already born?

Is our home or our income too small to cope with family needs?

What is our mutual response to birth control?

What roles are we fulfilling—and how effectively—in marriage and family?

Have we considered Church-approved methods of birth control?

Would contraception promote a responsible and fulfilling Christian relationship between us?

What is its meaning in our relationship and in our family life?

Increasingly, Catholics are reacting against the automatic assumption that the more children the better the marriage and family. That assumption overlooks the subjective dimension that goes along with the objective facts. What are the motivation and intention behind a large family? There are couples who have serious problems with intimacy and so they have another baby to avoid their problems. This provides an outlet for their emotions and their feelings and a sense of justification for them as parents of a large family. But have they examined their relationship and the values that are involved in their decision?

The couple may be taking the heat off the relationship by having another child. Instead of expressing a positive value, another child can mean another evasion. At some point, such evasion no longer works; more problems are created than solved. A crisis could come in terms of children's behavior, in the way the couple deal with each other or with individual problems, such as drinking.

To consider this an argument for or against large families is to miss the point that needs to be made. Both subjective and objective dimensions are involved in moral acts. To automatically obey or disobey Church law is to evade the responsibility of deciding. It is too easy to practice birth control "because everyone else is doing it and says it's all right," just as it is too easy to say: "Of course, we won't use the pill because the Church says it's wrong."

Still, guilt can creep in between the cracks when we make up our conscience. With all deliberate attention to the morality of a decision, self-doubt can emerge, with guilt not far behind. Certainly, each moral decision is individual, but we are still part of our environment and we do benefit and/or suffer, depending on the reaction of significant others.

Getting outside ourselves helps. Talking about our decisions can give us perspective by placing the decision out there where we can get a better look. Usually, someone else—mate, relative, friend, confidante—

can help us to sort out feeling, hangup, information, judgment. Someone else often notices something we are blocking or helps us to identify a significant factor. Bottling up doubts and guilt feelings can be destructive as well as misleading.

But we can't be indiscriminate about discussing decisions. We need to trust and respect the other person. We need a sense of the other's pre-judgments and assumptions. In particular, we should be confident that the other person listens, really listens to us. We should not be misled by the kind of listener whom Professor Bergen Evans of Northwestern University has described as lying in wait to pick up the thread of his or her discourse "that the other person rudely interrupted."

The useful listener pays attention to the entire person, to feelings as well as facts, to emotions as well as ideas. Such a listener *communicates* interest and curiosity not by mouthing platitudes but by being present to the situation and by not interrupting or rushing to judge. Active listening means standing in another's shoes and making the effort to get inside another's situation.

For Catholics, the priest, particularly in the role of confessor, is a special confidante on moral decisions. And a good confessor is, above all, a good listener. Such a confessor hears not only words spoken but the feelings, attitudes, and disposition behind the words. He realizes that people don't always say what they mean in words, but can get their message across in tone of voice, gesture, expression. He senses shyness and nervousness as blocks to communication and he avoids sounding like a judge who is rushing to judgment. The priest's task is to work toward understanding—not to play God by passing judgment.

The new rite makes this clear by stressing a dialogue between priest and penitent. Memorized formulas are no longer necessary; the penitent no longer has to enter defensively and announce, "Bless me, Father, for I have sinned." More significantly, the sacrament now provides for a face-to-face encounter where the penitent is no longer a disembodied voice and the priest a shadowy figure. In the past, that has led to a situation where confessors seemed to be dealing with "a brain on stilts." Now the rite emphasizes that the whole person is involved—on both sides.

The priest—whether confessor or counselor—is in the role of helping the individual to make up his or her mind, not in the position of telling another person what to do. He helps us to face the question: What do we want? He does this by bringing information, perspective, and Church teaching into the picture.

An example will show how question-asking enters into moral decision-making. A middle-aged family man becomes involved in an affair with a young woman at his office. He has five children, a devoted wife of more than twenty years—and a problem. He is on the brink of leaving his wife and family and going off to marry this woman. He comes to the priest to discuss his problem. Here's what the priest may say to himself in his role as counselor:

I want to give him pastoral compassion. I want to try to *feel* for him, to sense his pain in making this difficult decision. I don't want to throw him down the steps of the rectory because he is involved in a situation that looks immoral to me. But at the same time I want to give him more than he would get from a corner bartender. I don't want to be so non-directive that I just reflect back all he says and all his feelings. I want to help him make an ethical decision. I'll never make that decision for him, but I will try to get him to look at the whole picture.

Questions can frame a moral issue. They reflect the double point of view on material and formal matter, objective and subjective sin. The questions include:

What kind of relationship is this? How deep is the commitment? Is this an infatuation? Are you reacting against a feeling that youth is gone and manhood on the wane? Are you being honest with this new love? Can your new relationship survive transplanting from the office setting? Is there sharing of two selves? Or is the relationship thriving mainly on the natural excitement of two people attracted toward each other? When you leave aside the excitement and the problems you must be discussing, what are you sharing?

What of your wife? What is the meaning of your marital vows? Have the two of you tried to work on your problems? Have you tried Marriage Encounter? Have you thought of family therapy? Have you tried to work with your wife on what you feel is lacking in the marriage? On second thought, are you running from problems in your current marriage into a new relationship where the same problems may arise? Will a new marriage with a new person mean a new and better relationship? What will a divorce do to your wife? To the children? Would it be better for your children if you stayed or if you left? What relationships would you like to have with your children in the future?

Should you wait? Should you try to find out more about yourself, your needs and desires as well as your problems? Do you need time alone to get more perspective? Should you try separation—from your wife or from your woman friend?

And, basically, the questions:

Who are you?

What do you want out of life?

Moral decision-making is by no means synonymous with decisions to sin or not to sin. To think of morality only in terms of violating the commandments or precepts, rules and regulations is to become enmeshed in negative "guilt" thinking. Morality is the pursuit of what is *good*, a pursuit that involves decision to act or not to act, to go in one direction or in another. Such decisions may have nothing to do with obligations. They may concern options, such as a lifetime choice and commitment.

Consider the example of a young man or woman weighing a religious vocation. The questions to ask in such a situation are really not significantly different from questions to be asked for any major moral decision.

What seems to be attracting me to this way of life?

Do I have a realistic view of it?

What would this commitment mean?

Have I weighed the sacrifices involved?

In the case of a religious vocation, have I weighed what is involved and whether I could live a satisfying life without a conjugal relationship?

What are my talents? My liabilities?

Am I willing to put the time and effort into the years of study and preparation?

On and on, the morally-responsible individual

strives and strains to sort out circumstances, personal values, and deeply-felt needs and beliefs—struggling to be honest about desire, motivation, and reasons, about himself or herself.

Whenever we turn to someone for counsel at such times of major decisions, the counselor is being called upon to play a meaningful role in our decision-making. There are questions to ask about the counselor, as well. In moral areas, a priest is typically the counselor sought out by Catholics, so questions can be framed to evaluate his role—bearing in mind that the questions really apply to any moral counselor. (Obviously, it is better to have a regular priest-confidant than to turn to one in times of crisis and pressure when it is more difficult to assess his value to us.)

Is the priest helping me to make progress in sorting out moral decisions on my own?

Is he helping me to handle these situations better than I have handled them in the past?

Is he more than a crutch who just says *yes* to everything I say? Or a critic who just waits for the chance to say *no*?

Is he challenging me to realize that sin is not the central theme of Christianity?

Is he working with me so I can recognize where I have failed in my responsibilities and working with me as I develop my Christian values?

Is he responding to all of me, not just to my problems?

By helping to clarify ethical stakes, the priest-counselor—or any other confidante—liberates us from unnecessary burdens while making us more aware of legitimate ones. This makes us freer of misguided and misplaced guilt, while contributing to the development of a mature conscience.

The effort goes on and on throughout our lives, pursuing moral questions and sharing, where appropriate, that pursuit with meaningful others. The effort, by its very nature, makes us less apt to sin and is an antidote to guilt. It works out this way:

Sin is separation from fellow humankind and from God.

Each individual asking how he or she can meet moral responsibilities is moving toward others, not away.

We are thereby answering the question: What do we want? We want union with humankind and with God. Sin, separation, guilt have no part in all this.

9
The Challenge of Guilt

Jacques Maritain has pointed out that "the only practical knowledge all men have naturally and infallibly in common is that we must do good and avoid evil."

Guilt confirms the point for Christians, offering emotional evidence that humans want in their deepest selves to be true to their humanness. This translates into the do-good, avoid-evil principle.

Conscience is the judge and jury that confront the evidence and the law. Depending on the verdict, the sentence is emotional pain or emotional satisfaction.

No Christian escapes this moral process, which, as we have discussed, places its burden basically on the individual. Guilt is always there to remind, to prod, and to punish. The challenge is to make guilt work for our moral lives and for our personal fulfillment rather than undermine our sense of self and cloud our turning toward others and to God. So, to repeat our argument, guilt cannot and should not be done away with. It should be dealt with. Guilt challenges us. It is the irritant that can produce pearls.

Whether we act or not, commit or omit, we must choose. To live is to choose—one way or the other. The consequences involve our feelings, among them, feelings of guilt or innocence. C. S. Lewis, who has written with insight about Christianity in the modern world, points out that "every time you make a choice you are turning the central part of you, the part of you that chooses, into something a little different from what it was before."

We are creating our own biographies, reading and reacting as we write them. Lewis focuses on that central part which makes choices: "And taking your life as a whole, with all your innumerable choices, all your life long you are slowly turning this central thing either into a heavenly creature or into a hellish creature: either into a creature that is in harmony with God, and with other creatures, and with itself, or else into one that is in a state of war and hatred with God, and with its fellow-creatures, and with itself. To be the one kind of creature is heaven: that is, it is joy and peace and knowledge and power. To be the other means madness, horror, idiocy, rage, impotence, and eternal loneliness. Each of us at each moment is progressing to the one state or the other."[1]

Guilt plays its part in that progress. It provides feedback. It is the feeling that seeks to separate good and bad. Rather than abolish guilt, we all benefit from it as a flashing sign in the continuous effort to:

1. Identify, differentiate, and pursue the values that arise from our fundamental option as Christians.

2. Understand the rules and laws emanating from the Church in terms of the values involved.

3. Integrate values and laws that come from all directions and to work toward making sense for ourselves out of this network of moral responsibility.

In such a context, guilt is not the motivation, and certainly should not be the controlling force.

The possibility of guilt comes with the realization

that freedom and responsibility go hand in hand. Because we can choose consciously between right and wrong, we are going to feel at odds with our own humanity when we choose what we consider wrong. The disharmony leaves us uneasy—feeling guilty.

The feeling also makes us sensitive to the consequences of our actions. That is the moral choice, coming out of the realization that we act in terms of our relationship to ourselves, to others, and to God. A certain amount of tension and stress is involved in acting out of individual responsibility. Someone else or some other authority—such as the Church—is not doing the choosing. We are choosing. We are responsible.

Rather than a negative, destructive force, guilt should be a source of creative tension, part of the dynamics of being a responsible Christian. As an integral part of the human experience, guilt has been central in the Christian tradition in the sense that penance, forgiveness, and compassion all imply an awareness of guilt. It is a reminder of human frailty, of what Mark Twain caught in an aphorism: "Man is the only animal that blushes. Or needs to."

Awareness of wrong-doing is a reminder of human limitations as well as responsibilities. It is an eye-opener. Such awareness signals the imperfect human struggle to do good and avoid evil. C. S. Lewis was particularly perceptive on this point: "When a man is getting better, he understands more and more clearly the evil that is still left in him. When a man is getting worse, he understands his own badness less and less. A moderately bad man knows he is not very good; a thoroughly bad man thinks he is all right. This is common sense, really. You understand sleep when you are awake, not while you are sleeping. . . . Good people know about both good and evil; bad people do not know about either."²

Guilt is integral to the two-sided human adventure: on one side, freedom; on the other, responsibility. In shortchanging our freedom, we fail in our responsibility. In exaggerating our freedom, we distort our responsibility. There is a lifelong tension here in which guilt gathers its emotional force as we come to realize: The individual is less free than we used to think, but more free than many people today are ready to acknowledge.

On the one hand, each person has the positive power—the will—to choose for himself or herself in spite of difficulties and obstacles. This has always been considered necessary for the humanly-responsible act—the ability to say *yes* or *no* freely. This does not involve degrees of freedom; it is the freedom *to*. It is what has always been meant by free will. (In moral theology, this is called philosophical freedom.)

On the other hand, psychological freedom involves pressures, obstacles, and stresses which constitute difficulties on the path of freedom. This does admit of degrees and is relative. The greater the obstacles and the more powerful the pressures, the less the facility to choose or to act. What is involved is greater or less facility of choice. It is freedom *from*—in addition to freedom *to*. Both are necessary for serious sin to be committed, both together are essential to understanding "full consent of the will."

All of us carry heavy psychological baggage which has been labeled "dynamic unconscious." We have buried deep beyond the recall of ordinary memory and awareness many feelings, impressions, and reactions. They shape, influence, and point us in certain directions without our taking them into account. (They are what Freud pursued in depth analysis in order to bring them to the surface.) They help to explain moods, prejudices, attitudes, and sometimes even reactions to authority. They influence serious life decisions, including choice of career, friends, mate. As Monden has pointed out, "normal" persons are not as free as they might wish to be; they don't always do what they want to do.

The point is captured in a parable about a little boy trapped on a sliver of beach between a rising tide and towering cliffs. He has nowhere to go as the water gets higher and higher around him. Suddenly, he spots a wooden crate and stands on top of it in order to keep his head above water. The tide rises and rises, reaching as high as his chin, then recedes, leaving him safe, relieved, and eager to get away from the place. He looks down at the crate that saved him and takes it along. In fact, he always keeps it by his side. It becomes part of him. He is afraid to go anywhere without it.

Twenty years later when we encounter him, still carrying the crate, we ask, "Why in the world are you carrying that crate around?"

"I don't know," he replies, "but I'm sure not going to let it go."

To continue with the parable, other "crates" are added by society, though he may not be aware of them. He is being constantly shaped by the culture he lives in, by the high tide of media messages rising all around him, by his peer group. Hidden persuaders abound, whether they are pressures to keep up with everyone else or to seek approval, affection, and esteem. In this sense, too, no person is an island. Because of what surrounds each person, freedom is weighed down by social realities.

Then there is the question in morality, "Did you realize fully?" (sufficient reflection). Knowledge of what we are doing is not enough. This cerebral, mental, rational knowledge must be linked to evaluative knowledge, appreciation, and awareness of what a choice signifies.

Thus, the problem of establishing the amount of freedom is compounded by the difficulty of clarifying awareness. It is clearly too rigid and narrow to say that such-and-such an action is always a sin. It is also too lenient and anarchic to say that such-and-such an action or choice is never a sin, especially in the light of merit and blame, pastoral practice, penance, the doctrine on sin and grace, redemption and salvation. Therefore:

Avoid *always* and avoid *never* in dealing with sin and guilt.

The average person is certainly free of moral guilt more frequently than the old view would admit, given the realities of freedom and awareness.

Each case must be decided on its own merits and very often we won't be certain even then.

So guilt and sin are not obsolete. What is happening is that they are being integrated into the entire life of the committed Catholic. They are the negative and dark side of the positive and bright side of the Christian life lived by the twofold commandment.

Our very concern about sin and guilt is a vindication, a reminder that we are engaged in the salvation story. When we examine sin and guilt in our lives, we can and should move beyond the shame and pain to the satisfaction that comes from pursuing a Christian life.

Notes

INTRO   1. Karl Menninger, M.D., *Whatever Became of Sin.* (New York: Hawthorn Books, 1973), pp. 1-2.

2. Interview with one of the authors. See "Futurechurch" by Edward Wakin, U.S. CATHOLIC January 1977.

3. E. F. Schumacher, *Small Is Beautiful* (New York: Harper & Row Perennial Library, 1975), p. 38.

4. E. F. Schumacher, *A Guide for the Perplexed* (New York: Harper & Row, 1977), p. 60.

5. Menninger, *op. cit.*, pp. 24, 188.

1   1. Ruth Benedict, *The Chrysanthemum and the Sword* (Boston: Houghton Mifflin Company, 1946), pp. 222-223.

2. David Reisman, with Nathan Glazer and Reuel Denney, *The Lonely Crowd* (Garden City, N.Y.: Doubleday Anchor Books, 1953), pp. 40-41.

3. *Ibid.*, p. 42.

4. Thomas Aquinas, *Summa Theologica*, II.

2   1. Thomas Merton, *No Man Is An Island* (New York: Dell Publishing Co., 1957), pp. 20-21.

2. Interview with one of the authors. See "To Have or To Be, That Is the Question" by Edward Wakin, U.S. CATHOLIC, June 1977.

3. Frank J. McNulty, *Invitation to Greatness* (Denville, N.J.: Dimension Books, 1974), p. 27.

4. Louis Monden, S.J., *Sin Liberty and Law* (Mission, Kansas: Sheed Andrews and McMeel, Inc., 1965), p. 130.

4   1. In describing the three levels of ethical conduct, we have drawn on a work that has become something of a classic among teachers of moral theology: Louis Monden, S.J., *Sin, Liberty and Law*, Sheed, Andrews and McMeel, 1965.

2. Erich Fromm, *To Have or To Be?* (New York: Harper & Row, 1976), p. 122.

3. Paul Tournier, *Guilt and Grace* (New York: Harper & Row, 1962), p. 90.

4. Merton, *op. cit.*, pp. 47-49.

5   1. "Conscience and Superego: A Key Distinction," John W. Glaser, S.J., *Theological Studies*, March 1971. p. 43. This influential article has been particularly useful as a source for the chapter.

9   1. C. S. Lewis, *Mere Christianity* (New York: Macmillan Paperbacks, 1960), pp. 86-87.

2. *Ibid.*, p. 87.